You Can't Get There From Here

YOU CAN'T GET THERE FROM HERE

The Story of Music Industry Promoter Vernice Watson's Rise—From the Radio Kings of the 60s to the Gospel Explosion of the 90s

by

Vernice Watson

with

Milton Allen

VERLEN PUBLISHING COMPANY
Baltimore, Maryland

Publishing History:

First Printing August 2000

Second Printing February 2001

Verlen Publishing Company, Baltimore 21208
© 2000 by Verlen Publishing and Vernice Watson
 All rights reserved
Printed in the United States of America

Interior design by Alan Bell

07 06 05 04 03 02 01 00 99 5 4 3 2 1
ISBN 1-892970-00-7

To my Dad.
For being such a special person in my life
and always teaching me
right from wrong.

Contents

ACKNOWLEDGEMENTS / IX

Chapter 1
BLACK RADIO REIGNS SUPREME / 1

Chapter 2
NOT JUST A JOB, AN ADVENTURE / 91

Chapter 3
THE DWARF VS. THE GIANT / 137

Chapter 4
THE LAWYERS / 157

Chapter 5
EPILOGUE / 189

Acknowledgements

When I first started writing this book, I wrote for revenge. I hated AT&T, and I hated what I had become because of the ill-fated events surrounding my ordeal with AT&T. I took God for granted.

During the writing process, I grew spiritually. I went from hating a corporate "giant" to appreciating the experience. I learned that my story as well as my life's work and experiences are a legacy to be shared.

I've gone from respecting my best friend to almost hating him, because at times he did not share the same passion I had for this book. But now I respect him and his talents more than ever. And I have a real love and respect for my family, Nichelle, Alvin, Stanley, Marnita, Paula, Jason, Najéa, Najhan, and my real friends (you know who you are).

Most of all, I love and respect God in a way that is different—

more honest and more sincere.

This volume would not have been possible without the trials, tribulations and successes I encountered working in the record industry. Similarly, it could not have been completed without the help, encouragement and expertise of a host of people.

I wish to acknowledge and thank each and every person I have come in contact with—good, bad, and indifferent—during and before the conception of *You Can't Get There From Here.* Each of you has been at the very core of this effort.* Special thanks also goes to:

Milton Allen, for hanging in there with me for what was a very difficult task.

Hazel Harrison and Linda Hughes, for taking my original manuscript and guiding me through it, forcing me to become a better writer.

Hank Mance, for giving me the idea and the inspiration to write this book in the first place.

Tina Stephens, for sitting up in bed at night and reading this really raw material and encouraging me to go on when I didn't know if I really had a book or not.

James Alexander, for reading those early pages, offering his constructive criticism and making me take out all the bad words.

Sidney Miller of *Black Radio Exclusive,* for his December 6, 1996 issue giving me my first review, even before it became a book.

Wayne Cooper, for encouraging me to do an audio version of the book, and who took me into the studio and made me realize that we needed to bring in Pat Prescott to do it right.

Pat Prescott, The Voice, for being a wonderful friend and making the audio version.

Vicki Mack Lataillade, for giving me the perfect ending for the book.

Tom Joyner, for the personal note of encouragement that helped me to go on.

Oggi, the premier DC record biz photographer for the last twenty years, without whom I would not have been able to capture many of the rich images portrayed in this book.

Ralph Nader and Wesley J. Smith, for writing the book *No Contest—Corporate Lawyers and the Perversion of Justice in America.*

More special thanks:

To those who gave interviews, provided recollections and gave their own special insight. You not only enhanced the book, you made the experience a joy by sharing your own unique perspectives about a very special time in my life and in the music business:

Troy Williams, Kwame Alexander, Vanessa Vaughn, Joyce Logan, Jack Gibson, Billie Love, Bobby Bennett, Curtis Anderson, Don Brooks, Sue Woods, Glynice Coleman, Tony Anderson, John Smith, Gentry McCrary, James Bullard, Doug Daniel, Jean Alston, Renee Brooks, Eilene Lifsey-Towns, April Washington, Jim Henry, Della Williamson, Queen Jones, Frances Jones, Pat G'Orge Walker, Casilda Dailey, Victoria Galvez, Jaquie Gibb, Ronnie Baker, Tim Watts, Tony Beck, Patrick Spencer, Waymon Jones, Kevin Evans, Michael Soward, Telisa Stinson, Sheila Eldridge, Jalila Larsuel, Vernon Simms, Denise Marcia, Maurice Starr, Bobby Blackwell, Bill Harvey, Peter J. Allen.

To those of you who provided encouragement and to those of you who without being there over the years, this story would not have been possible:

Patrick Ellis, Jacquie Gales Webb, Donnie Simpson, Lee Michaels, Bishop Naomi Durant, Cathy Hughes, Jeff Majors, B. Berry, Lou Hankins, Bishop Louise Williams, Cody Anderson, Joe "Butterball" Tamburro, Rick Green, Chris Squires, Diane Brown, Eunice "Neicy" Tribbett, Linda Timmons, Sam Williams, Percy Williams, Fred Handy, Fred Blain, Donna Wilson, Alphie Williams, Robyn Holden, Duane Johnson, Kweisi Mfume, Reggie Utley, Dianne Blackmon-Bailey, Sonya Love, Lisa Collins, Raynetta Ray, Lenair Holton, Connie Flint, Juandolyn Stokes, Jacquie Hasslerig, Taft Harris, Pam Morris, Felecia Kampbell, Al Hobbs, Cavell Phillips, Doc Christian, Hardy Jay Lang, Leon Toller, Robert Wilson, Don Allen, Sr., Don Allen, Jr., Kris McCoy, Deborah Smith-Pollard, Tim Smith, Martha Jean (The Queen) Steinberg, Kenneth Robinson, Othor Cain, Freddie Rhodes, Dale Edwards, Ruby Summerville Dickson, Bobby Jones, James Chambers, Tracy Bethea, Michael McKinney, Clarence Kilcrease, Jerome Thomas, Larita Winston, Bill White, Ray Edwards.

—*Vernice Watson*

You Can't Get There From Here

Chapter 1

Black Radio Reigns Supreme

It was 1975—an incredible time to be in the radio and record business. The record business was booming. It had been enjoying a steady period of unparalleled growth. Much of that growth was fueled by unprecedented music sales by Black artists. Sales records were being set by Earth, Wind & Fire, Parliament/Funkadelic, The Commodores, Motown and Philadelphia International Records. Black Music had made such an impact on corporate bottom lines that the major record companies had formed Black "divisions" to make the music and promote the records. The initial talent pool for these new divisions came right out of Black radio. Successful programmers like Paul "Fat Daddy" Johnson from WWIN in Baltimore and Cortez Thompson from WOL in Washington became Vice Presidents of Promotion. By the mid-seventies, record companies needed a new infusion of talented and creative middle managers to fill their ranks. We were the new blood. We had great respect for the Black professionals that trailblazed the path for us. But now it was our time—and we've dominated the executive corridors of record companies ever since.

Black radio dominated the airwaves with powerhouse AM stations like WOL in Washington, WWIN in Baltimore and WDAS in Philadelphia. In the early seventies, there had also been a not-so-quiet revolution going on in Black radio. Black FM stations had hit the airwaves and taken the market by storm. WHUR-FM, owned by Howard University in Washington, DC, WDAS-FM in Philadelphia and Inner City Broadcasting's WBLS in New York, were playing albums and expanding Black radio programming beyond the top 40 playlists of their AM brethren. These stations began to change the way Black music was programmed and sold. They were playing jazz, funk, soul, reggae, blues and gospel. As a result, more albums were sold by Black artists than ever before in the history of the music industry. In 1975, it was not unusual to hear *P-Funk* by Parliament, Van McCoy's *Hustle*, Earth, Wind & Fire's *Shining Star*, Roy Ayers' *Everybody Loves the Sunshine*, War's *Why Can't We Be Friends?*, The Temptations' *A Song for You*, The O'Jays' *I Love Music*, Harold Melvin and the Blue Notes' *Bad Luck*, George Benson's *This Masquerade*, Bob Marley's *Natty Dread* and Grover Washington Jr.'s *Mister Magic*—all on the same FM station.

The disc jockeys, music directors and program directors became power brokers. They held the fortunes of multi-million dollar record companies in their hands (or more specifically, on their turntables). They were like little kings ruling over their individual kingdoms. And rule they did. A free for all resulted, with the record companies supporting whatever the "Kings" wanted.

In those days, the record companies lined up to dole out payola to disc jockeys and programmers to insure that their records were played. It was something that was never discussed, just done. Record company reps or independent promoters handled the chore of doling out favors, sex, drugs or direct cash payments.

Record companies, especially the independently distributed labels, would ship commercial copies of product known as "cleans" to their promotion people. These were for-sale copies that were the currency of the music business. The words "cleans" and "cash" were synonymous. Sales of "cleans" generated cash money for radio payoffs. It was a nice, neat little system. Any one-stop (a sub-distributor that sold to smaller, mom and pop retail accounts) would not mind buying clean product from promotion people at a reduced price because anything they didn't sell would be returned to the distributor and then ultimately to the record company. No wonder a lot of the small independents are now out of business.

It even got to the point where some of the more enterprising dee jays became concert promoters—making crazy money. What a great deal they had. In exchange for getting their records played, the record companies gave the kings the acts, and the kings would keep all the money. Unfortunately, that practice ultimately become their undoing. But that's another story for someone else to tell.

I remember attending the National Association of Television and Radio Artists (NATRA) conventions and testimonial dinners, which to me were just veiled vehicles to dole out more favors, payola and good times for the people that really counted in the music business—*the Black radio kings*. That was the backdrop for my introduction into the record business.

NATRA

Charles Anson, the current Executive Director of Public Relations for the Maryland State Lottery, was the "overnight man" at the now legendary WOL radio. Back then, he was known as "Mr. C." The overnight man was the disc jockey who worked what we called the graveyard shift, usually from midnight to 5 A.M. or 2 A.M. until 6 in the morning. The graveyard shift was also a time when record promoters would take a respite at radio stations, entertain the overnight jocks, and get their records played while no one was around.

I remember the first time I met Charles and several of his friends—DC players, of course. In those days a "player" was a single guy with a job. He was usually handsome and well dressed. Who could ask for anything more? My girlfriends Norma, Shirley, Jasmin and I were on our way up to the Playboy Club Hotel Resort at Great Gorge, a beautiful resort located in the mountains about 50 miles northwest of New York City. Great Gorge was the flagship of the Playboy universe. It was everything the Playboy Club represented. The entire Playboy philosophy could be encapsulated in this one place. It had everything from a full golf course, horseback riding, tennis, swimming, workout rooms, great nightclubs and discos. And to enjoy it, you had to have plenty of money!

We met Charles and his friends at the exclusive Marbury Plaza condominiums in southwest Washington for the annual fall trip to the club. It was a wonderful drive. I'll never forget listening to Patti Labelle's *Isn't It a Shame* while watching the brilliant colors of the autumn leaves at sunset as we cruised up the New Jersey highways. What should have been a six-hour drive turned out to be ten hours. The co-pilots in the lead car fell asleep and missed the most important turn, McAfee, N.J. We finally got there! It took so long, we called it the "Playboy Club Wagon Train." We were all just players hanging out in the mountains at the fabulous Playboy Club Resort. I was having a ball and I ended up hanging out with "Mr. C" and his friends every weekend.

Charles had a nice lifestyle. He had two homes in Annapolis—a townhouse, summer home, and a boat. Charles was a fun person to be around. The fact that he was a big-time disc jockey did not really faze me—he was just a good friend and a nice guy. These radio and record people were really very interesting. They had a very casual, even cynical outlook on life; most of them seemed to work only a few hours a day. Yet they all seemed to live very well. They partied harder than any group of people I had ever encountered. That was one thing they all had in common.

One Friday night we went out to dinner in DC with some friends, and Charles said, "Let's ride over to Baltimore to check out this convention."

I wondered to myself, *What in the world are we going to do at a convention at 11 o'clock at night?* What I saw that night made a permanent change in my life.

We got there about midnight. Electricity was in the air, the people were energetic and alive, the atmosphere was exciting. At the time, I was a mental health counselor at Provident, a Black-owned hospital, and I taught classes for the Motor Vehicle Administration. I was used to dealing with crazy people. But *these* people were outrageous. And they were having big fun.

We went from suite to suite where different groups of people danced, drank and partied. Posters hung on the walls. A different record company hosted each suite. Each company played its new music. All the suites had open bars with top-shelf liquor and lavish spreads of food. Each tried to outdo the other.

I remember having to step over one guy who was totally out of it. In some of the suites there was something going on in the back room behind a guarded door. I wondered, *What are they doing back there?* It was like a whole new world for me.

As the night wore on, our group went traipsing from suite to suite. It grew late, but the intensity didn't let up. We went to the Atlantic Records suite, and Charles was talking to some guy who he said wanted to meet me. Over the din of loud music, loud talking, laughter and clinking glasses Charles whispered to me, "You ought to meet this guy. He's got a house longer than the Civic Center.

"Vernice, I want you to meet Bill Anderson. He's what we call a 'Big Nigger' in the business," Charles said.

From what I could gather, Bill was called an "independent promoter," someone who promotes records for different record companies on a contract basis. It was well known that most of the payola was passed to programmers and disc jockeys through independent promoters. Bill never discussed it with me, but *whatever* he did, he sure had a rather extravagant lifestyle.

I talked to him and we hit it off, but I never gave him my number. Apparently, Bill had tried to get in touch with me, but as things went in those days with WOL, Charles blocked any contact until he got what *he* wanted. Then he gave Bill my phone number. Three months later, we started dating.

It was my first record business romance. After a few dates, my new friend said he wanted me to help him monitor radio. In other words, my job was to listen to radio stations and log the times they played his records. At the time, I lived in Silver Spring, Maryland, right outside of Washington, and I worked in Baltimore. I could monitor stations in both markets. I suspected he had been paying off dee jays in Baltimore and Washington, and since he wasn't in the area, he needed to make sure his records were being played.

As I look back on it, NATRA was probably responsible for bringing a lot of people into the record business, not based on seminars or panels, but on the parties. NATRA probably had the biggest P.Q. (party quotient) of any organization in history.

My friend Pat Prescott of WQCD in New York was a school teacher in New Orleans when she attended a NATRA Convention as a hostess. Pat saw how much money was being spent, but she wasn't particularly impressed by the caliber of people. In Pat's words, "Hey, if they can make all that money, so can I."

After that, she enrolled in one of those broadcast schools where you learn how to fix radios and got her first radio job on WYLD-FM in New Orleans. Today, Pat is the *only* female in New York radio to lead her own morning show. A leading industry trade magazine, *Radio & Records,* calls Pat "WQCD/New York's legendary morning personality"—thanks, in part, to NATRA.

It was 1976, and I was gradually becoming exposed to the music business. I went to Philadelphia for a testimonial dinner for Georgie Woods, one of the Philadelphia radio kings. The dinner looked like a Philly version of NATRA. Record executives flew in for this event. Even the Mayor was there. The event was impressive, but the people were of a different breed—or at least they *thought* they were.

People in the record business all seem to have a bad case of "terminal uniqueness." Lucky for me, my background as a mental health counselor helped me stay grounded in reality and to view people in the music business objectively. I always wondered, *What would these people be like if they were drug and alcohol free?*

At the dinner, we sat at a table reserved for Nashboro Records. Bill introduced me to Rick Magruder, Vice President of Promotion for Nashboro and Abet Records. He was a gracious table host. He and Bill seemed to have mutual respect and admiration for one another. Bill apparently worked for Magruder, but theirs was a symbiotic relationship. Neither man could get along without the other.

Publicly, they professed all this great respect for one another, but privately they talked about each other like dogs. It was a weird relationship, to say the least. My thinking is, if you despise someone so much, then don't work for them. But, like I said, they needed each other.

I tried to impress Magruder with what knowledge I had

picked up, and I just faked the rest. Rick and I talked for a while, and he told me he had an opening for a local promotion manager for the Baltimore-Washington area. I remember thinking to myself, *Is this man offering me a job?* All I could think about was the daughter I had to take care of and my two jobs. I wasn't so sure about the record business, so I called one of my friends, Phil Mathis, who told me, "You have *two* jobs. You can always get another job, but this could develop into a career." That was some of the best advice I've ever gotten.

So I said "yes" to Magruder, but I've got news for you. I didn't quit my day job. I worked as a mental health counselor and taught alcohol and drug education classes for the Motor Vehicle Administration from 3 P.M. to 9 P.M., and I worked for Nashboro Records. I did all this and took care of my daughter, Nichelle, too.

The Kings and I

The most basic duty of a promotion person is to get records played. The formula is very simple: No airplay equals no sales; therefore, no sales equals no job. A promotion man represents the record company to the radio stations. When a promoter goes to a radio station, his primary duty is to influence the decision-making process of the person or persons that determine the music playlist—*by any means necessary.* Most R&B (rhythm & blues) radio stations, as they were called in those days, received about 50 or more new releases per week but would only add from three to five records a week to their playlists. The financial fortunes of the record divisions of large corporations such as

Warner Brothers, United Artists and CBS were on the line, which accounted for an extremely competitive atmosphere and a lot of pressure on promotion people.

Record promotion people had to be resourceful, energetic, likable, diligent and creative. Conventional methods for promoting records included providing programmers with copies of new releases, information on sales, and trade magazine chart positions such as *Billboard, Cashbox,* and the now defunct *Record World.* There were other ways of influencing programmers' music decisions. Promoters spent a lot of time cozying up to retail buyers at record stores to get them to give their records favorable sales reports to radio stations. Sometimes this would involve giving away free records or even small gifts or favors to counter clerks at stores.

Promotion people were also responsible for setting up local promotional tours when recording artists came to town. They were responsible for escorting the artist around town or babysitting, depending on the artist. They hosted luncheons and dinner parties in the artist's honor and doled out the coveted concert tickets when the artist appeared.

Perhaps the record promoter is best known for the unconventional means of promoting records which, in the mid-seventies, included giving out payola (I'll pay, you play), drugs, women or men (all the programmers were men in those days), or whatever it took to get those records played. I never knew how widespread these practices were. I do know that, for the most part, promoters who worked directly for the labels didn't get involved in the seedier activities. The record companies used independents to do their dirty work for them while they turned their backs and acted as if they didn't know what was going on. In turn, the independents got rich, and the radio people were kept happy.

In the gospel world, we never did any of that stuff, or I should say, *I don't think we did*. For the most part, I always relied on the quality of the music I was promoting, relationships I had established, and the strength of my character to get records played. *Right! Even I had to laugh a little when writing this.*

WOL

There was nothing like record day at WOL. Every week, all the major promotion people and independents would line up to see Cortez Thompson, WOL's program director. Cortez was tall, about 6'3", fair complexion, with light sandy hair—a very nice looking guy. He could be very nice, but he was not to be played with. One by one they went in, and they either came out with a big smile, or they looked totally dejected and shaken. Most of the time it was the latter, because Cortez was a real hell-raiser. He terrorized people. My personal nickname for him was "The Golden Terror."

If you sat close enough to his door, you could hear him yelling and screaming. It was a weekly terror session for some people. I personally never had a problem with Cortez. I actually liked going to WOL, because I learned so much from listening to the promotion people, from the major labels and the independents.

I sat and listened to the conversations of people like Buddy Dee (Atlantic Records), Chappy James (Motown), Karen Chambers (Columbia), "Swinging" Sam Beasley (Atlantic Records),

Barry Terry (Warner Brothers), Max Kidd (Independent), Gwen Franklin (Casablanca), Zeke Zanders (Ariola) and, of course, the Gold Dust Twins, Gerald Bowie and Vernon Thomas (Schwartz Brothers). I never really had any formal training in the record business. I had to pick it up on my own. WOL was like a classroom for me.

When I first started going to radio, I had to act as though I knew what I was doing until I figured it out. I remember trying to figure out what the expression *"Billboard* with a bullet" meant. I was in the business for some time before I learned how the *Billboard* chart works. *Billboard* magazine was, and still is, the Holy Grail of the record business. The *Billboard* chart measured how well your record did at radio and retail nationally. The magazine's weighted system applied a certain number of points for reports from retailers and from radio stations. So if you were able to tell a program director that your record was "number 36 with a bullet" on *Billboard's* chart, that was good. The "bullet" represented upward momentum.

When I looked in *Billboard*, there were no bullets. There were *stars* next to certain numbers, so why didn't they say "number 36 with a star?" It made no sense to me at all when I first got started. Mind you, I didn't figure everything out on my own.

My next real friend in the business was Clayton Tucker. He was the regional promotion man for a major record label. He taught me a lot. He taught me the basics of the business. He taught me not only how things worked in the record business, but why they worked the way they did. Clayton was a wonderful friend, and ours was a relationship I will always cherish.

He taught me how to schedule my retail calls. We would call

our Baltimore stores on Monday, because the Baltimore stations called stores on Tuesdays. On Thursdays, we made calls to the Washington stores, because the radio stations called for their store reports on Fridays. Basic stuff.

But I really began to figure out the inter-connectivity between radio, retail and charts when I realized it was possible to actually manipulate the *Billboard* charts by influencing store reports. In the late 70's, when a record first came on the chart, radio points figured more prominently in the equation. Unless it was a superstar blockbuster release, retail didn't really come into play. However, as a record moved up the chart, retail points weighed heavier. From about #15 on up, retail reports virtually propelled a record up the charts. *Billboard* used to send out a sheet to their retail reporters every week. The reporters were supposed to fill in a blank next to each record to indicate how or whether a record was selling.

So it was quite simple. Based on the close relationship I had formed with retailers in my area, I would call and ask for a good report on my records every week. Some stores even allowed some promoters to fill out their *Billboard* report forms as long as they didn't exaggerate too much. If you did this all over the country, it was possible to manipulate the charts. No system was foolproof.

Nowadays, technology has taken over. We have Soundscan, a reporting system that actually monitors retail sales scans. And we have BDS, a system of electronically monitoring airplay. The system is virtually untouchable. To work a record today, you must go back to the basics. There are no shortcuts. Your database has to include all the important record distributors, chain stores like Musicland, and mom and pop stores across the country. You have to work those stores just like you work radio stations. You have to generate in-store play, and you have to advertise. But the bottom line is, all of that won't make a bit of difference if the record is no good. As Berry Gordy founder of Motown said, "It's what's in the grooves that counts." And believe me, if it isn't "in the grooves," you can bet you will eat those records later in the form of "returns"—the most hated term in the record business.

RECORD BUSINESS ECONOMICS 101

Another good friend of mine in the business, Barry Terry, the regional promo man for Warner Brothers Records, taught me a lot. Once, when we were on the road, I began pulling records out of my trunk. All of sudden Barry said, "Wait, these are cleans!"

"What in the world are 'cleans?'" I asked? I was constantly learning new things, and this was my lesson in Record Economics 101.

"'Cleans' are records not designated for 'promotional use only.' They have no extra holes, no cut corners and no promotional stamps or stickers," I was told. In other words, they are records you can sell. I used to give away cleans. That is a no-no. Cleans are the lifeblood of promotion.

Records are sold on consignment. Anything that doesn't sell can be returned. It's like a chain reaction. In independent distribution, the manufacturer sells the records to the distributor with payment due in 90 days. The distributor sells records to the one-stop (sub distributor) or retailers, with payment due in 30 days. If a record doesn't sell, it gets returned and eventually winds up back with the manufacturer somewhere.

Let's Make A Deal

There are two sides to the record business. There's the up side—the flash, the glamour, the trade magazines and the shows. Then there's the underside—the payola, dumping records, and returns—substance that goes straight to the bottom line. The record business is truly a study in duality, both in people and in practice.

Working for a small independent label, you didn't have the opportunity to "dump" records on a grand scale like promotion people who worked for the majors, or better still, for large independents. The independents were much more flexible when it came to getting access to product to do whatever it was you had to do. Product never leaves a trail. It's really very simple—you obtain the product (the hard part); you take it to a one-stop, you get money. You do what you have to do. I guess that is just one part of the business I missed out on.

I've got to tell you this story before I go on. A good friend of mine, whom we'll call John, worked for a large independent. Whenever I went over to his house, he had records stacked from floor to ceiling. I remember telling him one day, "This looks like the Schwartz Brothers' warehouse." Turns out, I wasn't far from wrong. At the time, John was selling more records out of his basement than his own distributor, Schwartz Brothers. *How could this be?*

It didn't seem like good business judgment to supply a promotion person with more clean product than your distributor. Turns out I was right again. Apparently, there were two disgruntled employees in the company's warehouse, former promotion men for the company. In the midst of a cutback, they were given the option of being fired or working in the company warehouse. This is how they got their revenge. They supplied John with clean product and split the proceeds.

When we went on the road together, John had two hotel luggage carts—one for his clothes and one for his records. He used to say, "When you're on the road, if you can't make at least $500 from dumping records, then don't take the trip." Keep in mind that $500 in 1975 is probably worth at least $1,500 dollars today.

I'll never forget the time he took a lot of records to an area one-stop. There were so many records it was scary. John told me not to worry, because the record was a hit and it would sell through. I argued that there was no way this amount of product would go undetected by Schwartz Brothers. But he assured me it would be all right, and there would be no trouble. Well, wouldn't you know it. Later that day, the Schwartz Brothers salesman walked in to this one-stop and was shocked to discover all these records by this particular manufacturer which he had been unable to sell to this particular one-stop. The salesman was incensed and started arguing with the owner—who promptly threw him out of the store.

Now just as bewildered as he was upset, the salesman went back to Jerry Jacobs, the sales manager at Schwartz Brothers, with his tale of woe. Jerry Jacobs assured the salesman he would call the label and "get to bottom of it." Jerry, being the veteran that he was, had seen this movie before. He knew this most likely would be a short-lived activity. All the records had come from the same place and they would all go back to the same place. In fact, depending on the situation, a few extra returns might help his balance sheet with his supplier.

Jerry also knew that there were three entities you did not want to raise problems with or create any static with. First was your supplier (the record company), second were your customers (the one-stops), and third was Jim Schwartz. Never, ever upset Jim Schwartz. So instead of calling the record company, Jerry phoned Schwartz Brothers' buyer and asked him to look into the situation. The buyer in turn called John. John told the buyer it was a one-time deal, made an "arrangement" with him, and it was all over. The buyer got back to Jerry saying it had been a one-time promotion thing—the guy needed money to pay dee jays. And that was it!

There was only one casualty in this whole story—the salesman. He was never allowed back into that account again. Then John made sure that he was labeled a snitch. I don't know what happened to that salesman, but I would be willing to bet that if he is still in the record business today, there are few who really trust him.

What's the moral of this story? Don't snitch, don't double-cross your suppliers, and most of all—don't ruffle your boss' feathers, especially if he's Jim Schwartz.

THE 360 DEGREE
TOTAL BLACK EXPERIENCE IN SOUND

WHUR was a totally different story from the established AM stations like WOL. When Howard University first started WHUR in 1971, the format was the "360 degree black experience in sound." They were revolutionary when it came to Black commercial radio.

WHUR played everything—jazz, R&B, Latin, reggae, gospel, you name it. The station even had the first female dee jays that I can remember on any format. They included Charlene Watts and my good friend and former roommate Alphie Williams. Alphie is now one of the top jocks at KDIA in Oakland, California. Later, WHUR would go on to hire female jocks Dyanna "Ebony Moonbeams" Williams, Robin Holden, and Sheila Eldridge.

Everybody listened to WHUR. They did things that were unheard of on Black radio stations, like staging live stereo concerts with Earth, Wind & Fire. WHUR sold concert tickets and albums by artists who had never gotten real exposure on the other R&B stations in Washington—WOL, WUST and WOOK.

WHUR broke so many new artists like Al Jarreau, Minnie Ripperton, Norman Connors and Phyllis Hyman, that it played a pivotal role in the way Black music was marketed, sold and recorded. In fact, it was the increased album sales resulting from Black FM airplay that made a fundamental shift in the economics and structure of the record business.

The sales base of Black product shifted from singles to albums. Self-contained groups like Earth, Wind & Fire, New Birth, WAR, Parliament/Funkadelic, and The Blackbyrds would not have been nearly as successful without the Black FM's going deeper into the albums and playing longer cuts than the AM stations single-oriented format would allow them to play. Contemporary jazz artists of the time like Donald Byrd *(Blackbyrd)*, Ramsey Lewis *(Sun Goddess)*, and Herbie Hancock saw a tremendous resurgence in popularity. Finally, traditional R&B artists began to stretch out with longer cuts and thematic albums. Marvin Gaye's *What's Goin' On* and Smokey Robinson's *The*

Quiet Storm were tremendous commercial successes, thanks to WHUR and all the Black FM formatted stations to follow.

This tremendous surge in album sales caused the record companies to wake up and pay attention to the Black consumer and to Black radio. As a result, the so called "autonomous" Black Divisions came into being, and a large infusion of Black people, mostly from radio, came into the employ of record companies. The architect of the WHUR sound was Andre Perry who started as the station's music director and eventually became program director. WHUR was the breeding ground for many music and radio industry professionals—most notably, Cathy Liggins, the former WHUR Sales and General Manager. Now she is Cathy Hughes, CEO of Radio One, the top Black owned and operated radio group in the country with stations in Atlanta, DC, Baltimore and Philadelphia.

By the time I started promoting records in 1976, WHUR's format had changed significantly. WHUR was more commercial, playing R&B. Jesse Fax was the music director and Oscar Fields was the music librarian. Jesse was a nice guy, tall with a beautiful smile. But he wasn't like the other music directors I knew. To me, Jesse Fax had the potential to be a promotion man's worst nightmare. He would never pay any attention to you. You would be in the music library doing your best pitch, and he would be reading the sports pages. I couldn't get anything out of this guy.

One day I was in there doing my thing. Jesse looked up from his box scores and said, "Why don't you tell your company to get some real records and stop bringing these dogs in here."

It just so happened that Jesse was right. Nashboro had great gospel product, but their R&B was pretty bad. Anyway, I told him he hurt my little feelings. I cried the blues, and I told him that my salary was the same every week whether he played the records or not. And I will never forget Jesse's response.

"Go tell your company it takes money to be in the record business, and if they don't have any, they need to go open up a candy store."

I've been using that line ever since.

Everybody in the record business is idiosyncratic, but Jesse Fax was just plain weird. His father was the Dean of Howard University School of Music. Jesse was really intelligent, but the only thing that seemed to interest him was buses—yes, as in transit buses—and old cowboy movies (he called them B movies). When New York City was in the midst of its fiscal crisis, Washington, DC, gave them about 100 buses. Jesse got so excited, he drove all the way up 95 and the New Jersey turnpike to "escort" the buses to New York City.

In June of 1978, I attended the BRE (Black Radio Exclusive) Convention in Los Angeles. The BRE was the convention to go to. Everyone who was anyone in the Black music business was there. You always had a great time, and you could take care of lots of business. This was the place where you could really showcase yourself. I would start preparing for the BRE in April by exercising, walking daily and eating the right foods to lose that winter weight. I would start thinking about what outfits I needed to buy, because you had to have several outfits—at least two per day. There were seminars, luncheons, dinners, showcases and concerts.

Perhaps the most important place at the BRE, however, was the lobby. That's where everybody congregated. To walk through the lobby sometimes took thirty minutes because there were so many people you wanted to talk to. It was a place to renew old relationships and create new ones. It was a relaxed atmosphere. We would take over an entire convention hotel, so you felt safe and insulated from the groupies, onlookers and the general public. You couldn't get into convention events without credentials, and sometimes not even into the hotel.

On the way to the BRE, I stopped in San Francisco for a couple of days to visit my mother-in-law, Fannie. I took some time for myself, being a tourist, taking in the sights, and shooting pictures. On the way to the Embarcadero, I saw a streetcar. I hadn't seen a street car since Baltimore got rid of them in 1967. I realized that this was something that Jesse Fax would get a real charge out of seeing. I photographed it, and the picture turned out great. I blew it up, mounted and framed it, then gave it to Jesse. He absolutely loved it. From that moment on, Jesse and I were the best of friends.

I developed some genuine relationships at WHUR. A promotion person gets to know people well. You find out their likes and dislikes. You find out the best way to deal with people to get the best results. When Eddie Lemon did the gospel shows, he liked traditional gospel artists like Shirley Caesar and James Cleveland. I would sit in the parking lot with fresh donuts and coffee at 5:30 a.m. waiting for Eddie to pull in. When AC (Anthony Carlton) did the gospel shows, he was more of a choir man.

I always knew WHUR was a gold mine in terms of generating album sales. Even though WHUR wasn't considered a major gospel outlet, I was in the market, and I could feel the impact of the station on gospel airplay. Many of the other record companies did not share my enthusiasm for WHUR.

When Patrick Ellis took over the gospel show in 1979, he didn't know anything about gospel music. He couldn't get service from a lot of labels. Jesse suggested that he give me a call. I turned Patrick on to a guy named Clarence who had a little combination record store and shoe repair shop up on 14th and Randolph in Northwest DC He did a lot of business in gospel—new and catalog. Clarence was one of those guys who was rich in knowledge about gospel. He knew the music, he knew the artists, the promoters, everybody. I figured that he could help Patrick out a bit. It wasn't until I was writing this book that Patrick told me he was always very grateful for the introduction, because Clarence helped him through the first three years and helped him really learn and understand gospel music. Now the WHUR gospel show is one of the most listened to gospel programs in the region and has been extended to two air shifts.

I met the station's other gospel announcer, Jacquie Gales Webb, years ago at Channel 9 TV in Washington when I brought Al Green over there on a promo tour. To this day we are very close.

Not long after I gave Jesse the streetcar, I was driving through Rock Creek Park in Washington. I remember thinking, *When are we going to have some real records, so I can stop promoting these bow-wows?* I heard Robin Holden, WHUR's popular mid-day dee jay play "*Wherever Your Love Goes*" by Skip Mahoney & The

Casuals. I flipped! I couldn't believe it! Jesse had actually added my record! There is nothing like the sensation that a promotion person gets when they hear their record on the radio for the very first time. I got chills when I heard it.

Everyday, no matter where I was at 2 P.M., I would have to start heading north to Baltimore to be at my motor vehicles job by three. Today was no different. Everybody in the record business knew I worked there; it was like my office inside of an office. As soon as I got to work the phone rang, and it was Candy Westerling, the music director at WKYS. Candy said she wanted to add Skip Mahoney & The Casuals. She wanted to play the "B" side instead of the "A" side, but who cares—it was still an add. And it was an add that I got and not my national or some independent! I had worked hard for that record. I even used to call the stations every day during drive time to request my record until they added it. The second best sensation a promotion person can have is calling your national office and reporting a new add.

I finally felt like a real promotion person.

Baltimore

Baltimore was mine. I was the promotion queen. I don't mean to say that I was the best, but I had excellent relationships with everyone—and relationships was what it was all about. At the time, all the promotion people in the area were either from DC or Philly. I was the only home girl who was doing promotion, and radio treated me like one of their own. I was one of them. I could talk about Johnny Unitas, Lenny Moore, the Baltimore Colts, the "white marble steps," Baltimore politics, the Lexington market—I was in there.

They all knew I had another job and a daughter, and they gave me a great deal of slack. I could walk into the radio stations anytime I wanted to. I was allowed to go into the control rooms. I could do just about anything I wanted. I considered them my friends: Kweisi Mfume, Program Director WEAA; Glynice Coleman and Curtis Anderson at WWIN; Dorothy Brunson; Pastor Naomi Durant; Don Brooks and Sue Woods of WEBB; and Pauline Wells Lewis of WSID.

WWIN—Where Kings Were Born and Legends Were Made

The title "kings" truly describes the radio personalities of Baltimore. "Legendary" does not adequately describe how great these people were, or their impact on the industry, Baltimore and me. We're talking about legends like Paul "Fat Daddy" Johnson; Maurice "Hot Rod" Hulbert; Rockin' Robin *(Give the bird some juice, go 'head and turn him loose; I want to see your face in the place, your feet under your seat and your smile as you walk down the aisle);* Diamond Jim Sears *(Hang loose and rock easy);* and Big Al Jefferson. When Al Jefferson was the program director at WWIN, he ruled WWIN, and WWIN ruled Baltimore.

Al Jefferson was the program director of WWIN after the legendary Paul "Fat Daddy" Johnson moved to the west coast for the greener pastures of Capitol Records. Fat Daddy was one of the first, if not *the* first, radio person to become head of a "Black" division of a major record label. It made sense. After all, who would understand the psyche of radio better than a successful radio man? Every time I see that Capitol Records tower in Hollywood, I think about Paul Johnson and Nat King Cole. I call it "The House That Nat Built." Forget the Beatles. If it hadn't been for Nat King Cole, there would probably never have been a Capitol Records label for Apple Records, the Beatles record company, to license their product for domestic distribution.

FAT DADDY: THE GREATEST OF THEM ALL

Anyway, I grew up listening to Fat Daddy saying "Good morning, Baltimore" on WWIN along with Al Jefferson, Kelson "Chop-Chop" Fisher, "Joltin' Joe" Parker, and Maurice "Hot Rod" Hulbert who coined such phrases as "Goodgoogala-moogala," "Get the nod from the rod," and "If it's the re-a-sod it's all re-a-zite."

Fat Daddy (Paul Johnson was his real name) was so ba-d-d, that virtually every year at the NATRA convention he won honors for Dee Jay of the Year. The man was so popular he actually put out his own records on the Chess label. In fact, it was an old album cover on one of his compilations I saw when I was a little girl that inspired the idea of the radio kings. The album cover pictured Fat Daddy with a crown, scepter and the other regalia that kings wear. It was tacky—some of that 60s stuff. But he looked like a king.

I remember my Aunt Georgie used to take me and my cousin Doris down to the world famous Royal Theater on Pennsylvania Avenue to see the stage shows. Fat Daddy would come out with a gold lamé cape and a crown. I remember saying to my cousin, "Look, Doris, he's a king." Even now, every year the most requested Christmas song in Baltimore is *Fat Daddy Santa Claus*, a record he actually recorded in his own voice:

> *I'm Fat Daddy*
> *(Sha na-na-na-naaa)*
> *From the North Pole*
> *(Woe woe yeah)*
> *I'm Fat Daddy*
> *(Sha na-na-na-naaa)*
> *Santa Claus with soul*
> *All the kids know me*
> *Simply because*
> *They know Fat Daddy is really Santa Claus*

Nowadays, you'd probably get fined or thrown in jail for putting out your own records and playing them on the air.

Each day, he would say "Good morning" to everyone: the milkmen, the crossing guards, the teachers, the postal workers, the Colts, the Orioles, you name it. It was a sense of community. Every morning. And we all listened. Fat Daddy had such command over the English language, and his voice was incredible. For years, I thought Fat Daddy had a newsman named Paul Johnson on his show, whom I assumed was White. I later found out that he would just change his voice come news time. Then he actually had conversations with himself on the air, between Fat Daddy and Paul Johnson. Everyone thought they were two different people. That's how good he was.

Fat Daddy's other mark was his use of words, rhyme and rhythm. He always used these four syllable words that no one ever heard of. It was kind of like ebonics, because even though you never heard the word before, you knew what it meant. During the NATRA conventions, Paul "Fat Daddy" Johnson held the audience spellbound with his elocution and verbal intrepidity. I believe the reason they kept giving him the award every year is just so they could hear him speak. I still think he made a lot of those words up. And I believe the group Parliament got that word "thrombipulation" right out of Fat Daddy's dictionary. It is ironic that a rhyme ended Fat Daddy's radio career and began Paul Johnson's record career. Fat Daddy was fired from WWIN for the furor that resulted when he said repeatedly: "The super-duper Supremes...make me —— —— my jeans."

Get the Nod from The Rod

Maurice "Hot Rod" Hulbert, passed in 1997. He was another master of elocution. "Goodgoogala-moogala," one of his catch phrases, has survived our parlance in various permutations over the years. He talked so fast, yet he spoke so clearly, he held the listener spellbound.

For years he put on a promotion called the "Hot Rod Tongue Twister." Anyone who could figure it out stood a chance to win money and prizes. He gave clues and enunciated sections of it slowly, but no one could ever figure it out. His other trademark was "VOSA," an acronym for the "voice of sound advice." I never knew what it meant until he passed. I thought it was just something he'd say, but he punctuated his statements with the term. A good example was his time i.d.:

> Time check, you bet Yvette,
> Big mommy-o's, big daddy-o's,
> Keen teens, ladies and gentlemen,
> Moo-moo's and birds,
> The time check is twenty-two minutes
> Before three o-clee-a-sod—VOS-A-H—H!

I got in big trouble because of Hot Rod. When I was in high school, Hot Rod had a promotion going on where if you showed up at the State Theater, you could audition to be one of his "Go-Go Girls." The State Theater was all the way on the east side of town on Monument Street near Johns Hopkins Hospital. If you won, your name would be announced on WWIN the next day, and you got to be one of Hot Rod's Go-Go girls, which meant you went to all of his dances and met a lot of people.

I was a good dancer, and I was determined to audition. I knew there was no way I was going to get permission to go. I remember my father specifically saying, "No daughter of mine is going to be a go-go girl up on stage shaking her butt." But that wouldn't stop me. I had already made up my mind I was going. I had it all planned.

One night my girlfriend Donna Davis and I were going to go to the State Theater. I took the clothes I was going to wear and threw them down the laundry chute so they would already be in the basement. This way, I didn't have to walk past my parents room with clothes in my hand. It was not unusual for me to go down into the basement at night to talk on the phone or do homework. So I went downstairs, took the basement phone off the hook, changed my clothes and climbed out the basement window. I walked all the way across the Forest Park Golf Course to Donna's house. We walked up to Gwynn Oak Avenue, about three quarters of a mile from my house, took the number 28 bus on Liberty Heights Avenue, transferred to the number 19 down Garrison Boulevard, and then to the number 13 on North Avenue all the way over to the forbidden eastside to Monument Street and the State Theater.

There were about 45 girls there. We were all up on stage, and Hot Rod explained the rules to us. Every time the music played, we danced, and whenever the music stopped, some of the girls were eliminated. It finally got down to me and nine other girls. I was nervous, but I was determined to win. And win I did! I reveled in the fact that my name would be announced on WWIN the next day at 4:00 and *all* my friends would hear, "Vernice Thorpe of Forest Park High School is a Hot Rod Go-Go Girl!"

Then we ran into a friend of ours who had taken his parent's car without their permission. We hopped in and had a good time laughing and joking all the way home. I was so happy. It was the most exciting thing that ever happened to me. On the way home it seemed as if my feet barely touched the ground. But when I got home, the laughing and the joking stopped. I knew I was in big trouble. I had the surprise of my life waiting for me.

The basement window was not only shut, it was locked. I knew that was my behind. I thought about running away from home, right there on the spot. *No, that wouldn't work, because I don't have enough money, and most importantly, I don't have my clothes,* I thought. I figured I was really too old to get a beating. After all, I was in high school. *Even if I did get a beating, maybe my father would do it instead of my mother. He always did it gently.* So I straightened up, rang the bell, and every light in the house came on. I knew this meant trouble.

My mother was absolutely enraged! She wore my butt out. I was on punishment for a whole year. I didn't get to dance as a Hot Rod Go-Go girl, but at least I heard my name on the radio, which means everyone heard it. Well I guess you could say I got "the nod from the 'rod.'"

"Big Al"

Unassuming and kind, Al Jefferson was the gentle giant of radio in Baltimore, Maryland. My Oliver Sain record *Party Hearty* had been #2 on the WWIN play list for six weeks; Big Al moved the record to #6. To me this was no big deal. After all, every record has to run its course. Six weeks at number two was as good as six weeks at number one as far as I was concerned. We were selling records like crazy in Baltimore. Milt Garland's Modern Music House, in Mondawmin Mall, Otto Burston's Your Record Shop, and Larry Dean and Eddie C's store on Edmondson Avenue were moving Oliver Sain records by box lots.

Two thirds of Mondawmin Mall, by the way, is owned by the Rouse Corporation, the people who built the city of Columbia (between Washington and Baltimore), the South Street Seaport in New York, and God knows what else. This little mall, built in the mid-fifties, is located in the heart of Black West Baltimore and does more business every year than 90 percent of the malls in this country.

Can you imagine? This little urban Mondawmin Mall is one of the top malls in the country, and that's a documented fact. That's how we knew when we had a record. When Milt Garland was pushing records out the door by box lots, you knew you had a hit on your hands. We've gotten away from that in the record business. Everything is scanners and computers now. If it's not scanned, it doesn't mean anything. If someone in the store doesn't drag that stupid little light over that bar code—it doesn't mean anything.

The heck with scanning. Let's get back to some good old-fashioned record selling. At one point in history, the store owner had his pulse on every record that was selling. He could "feel" it. But not anymore. Now, when you ask them how your record is doing, they've got to look at the scanning report. Give me a break.

As for my record dropping, at first it appeared to be a typical week. I called in my Thursday tracking with the new numbers—no big deal. The next morning, I remember looking at the clock—it was 8:10 A.M.—and the phone was ringing off the hook. *Who in the world is calling me this time of morning?* I said to myself. I picked up the phone, and it was Magruder yelling and screaming about that stupid record dropping to #6. I shouldn't have answered the phone. I knew better. Clayton always taught me that a good promotion person should be out the door by 8:30. Or at least that's what you want your bosses to think. (Remember, this was before caller i.d., voice mail, and even answering machines, which were expensive items and not widely used like they are today.) So I was caught.

I just held the phone away from my ear. I said nothing as I endured Magruder's verbal abuse. He went ballistic on me. When he screamed, he *really screamed*. Magruder insisted I go over to WWIN right away and demand that Al Jefferson move that record back up their playlist. He went on and on and on. Finally, I told Magruder, "No problem. I'll go see him, and I'll call you from the station."

After he hung up, I started thinking about the situation. First of all, I was grateful the record had been #2 for six weeks. Second, I had a good relationship with Al Jefferson, which I did not want to jeopardize. And third, it was Thursday— not Monday (Music Day). So you know I was not driving 90 miles round trip, and it's not even Music Day. So I called Al and told him about my little problem, and he said, " Please! Tell your *boss* to call *me*; I do the play list at WWIN radio. You did your job when you brought me the record. Tell him to call *me!*"

I gave Magruder the message, and that was the end of it. I don't know what happened in that conversation, but the record maintained good rotation for weeks on WWIN, even as it moved down the play list. In those days, program directors (PDs) had juice. They really did have the power to make or break a record. Nowadays, research makes or breaks a record. PD's could help you keep a job or lose a job. They could make careers or break them.

I went back to bed.

I learned that from the veteran promotion people—don't take it personal. Take a mental health day, and just go back to bed. When I first got into the business, I used to spend a lot of time feeling stressed out over these records. Then I realized that I had been taught by the very best. And as long as I did my job and did it well, with integrity, that's all that was necessary. So I stopped tripping off records, bosses that like to scream and artists that have yet to realize this is a business. That's when I developed a "no nonsense" attitude, and eventually a "no nonsense" reputation.

Speaking of the best, my friend Barry Terry, the mid-Atlantic regional promotion person for Warner Brothers, used to work for screamers like Harold Burnside. Barry said, "I'd be watching Monday night football, and Harold would call screaming about a record." Barry taught me a valuable lesson as he continued to explain, "When your national or VP screams, you scream louder. For example, when your boss says WWIN dropped the record, then you say, 'That common #@+*>&!$ lying so-in-so !&#@#*! I'm going to go in there tomorrow and kick his a—!' Now, you know you are not going to kick anybody's anything. But as a result of that little exchange, you got what you wanted. Your VP is happy because he thinks you are upset and that he has ruined your night. Then you go back to the game."

The key is, you scream louder. You make him or her believe you are even more upset than they are.

PASTOR DURANT HOLDS COURT

Pastor Naomi Durant from WEBB was something else! She had personality and panache. She drove around in a white Rolls Royce and was the kind of person who commanded the attention of all when she walked into a room. She used to have these awesome dinner parties at her Pikesville mansion which was formerly owned by one of Baltimore's first Jewish families.

It was a beautiful, huge house surrounded by rolling hills and mature trees. She was so proud of her renovations, she would take us on little tours of the house and the grounds. There was an old country kitchen and fireplaces in the living room, den and master bedroom suite. In the formal dining room she had two tables—a long table and a smaller round table. Both had plush high-backed seats. Because she would have name tags before your place setting, you always knew where to sit. The guest of honor and the important people sat at the long table, and the not-so-important ones sat at the round table. If you were at the main table, you were in high cotton. I was always at the main table.

Every time the Pilgrim Jubilee Singers or the Mighty Clouds of Joy, Alex Bradford or any major artists would come to town, she would throw one of these lavish dinner parties. She had a great soul food chef and server. The style was elegant, but not pretentious, lavish, yet simple. With Pastor Durant, it didn't make any difference what station you were from, we were all friends.

Kitty Broady and Pauline Wells Lewis were there from WSID along with Mary Clayborne from WWIN. Even Dorothy Brunson, the owner of WEBB used to come. Before buying WEBB, Dorothy Brunson was the general manager of Inner City Broadcasting's WBLS-FM and WLIB in New York. We would trade funny industry stories at that table. Ms. Brunson would captivate us with rich stories about New York radio, like the time Frankie Crocker, the legendary PD for WBLS in New York, allegedly got his legs broken.

It was fun and a true learning experience hanging out with Pastor Durant and Baltimore's best.

Kweisi Mfume

Kweisi was really the first of the "new school" dee jays in Baltimore. He was young, thought he was fine and had an afro-centric name. He played jazz on Sundays on WEBB. The station, a daytimer that operated from sun up to sun down, was 85 percent R&B. The rest was gospel. To say the least, jazz on WEBB at the time was considered revolutionary. Kweisi was a protegee of the legendary "Diamond Jim" Sears who, at that time, was the general manager for WEBB which was owned by the "Godfather of Soul" himself, James Brown. In Kweisi's inauguration speech for his job as CEO of the NAACP, he said Jim Sears was a second father, and he credits Diamond Jim with saving his life—from the streets of Baltimore. Diamond Jim used to say "Have mercy," and when he signed off the air he would always say, "Hang loose and rock easy."

Kweisi and I got to be very close friends. He emceed the very first show I promoted at O'Dell's, a popular Baltimore night spot, with my girlfriends Renee Brooks and Gloria Scott. (For a while I had fancied myself a concert promoter, and I actually made some money.) The show featured Skip Mahoney & The Casuals, my top R&B act from Nashboro's Abet label, and two local acts, Rhonda Milton, and Black Gold. (Bobby Blackwell, one of the former members of Black Gold, was my former across-the-street neighbor. He now owns the company that manufactures my *You Can't Get There From Here* tee shirts.

It was the summer of 1978. Kweisi had been the PD of WEAA, Morgan State University's station, since it first went on the air in 1977. He told me privately that he was thinking about running for office. Ever since 1970 when Milton B. Allen, Sr. became the first Black person to win a city-wide election, becoming the nation's first Black elected state's attorney, Baltimore had been a hotbed of political activity. If Kweisi ran, he would face the well entrenched incumbent, Victorine Q. Adams, who had been a fixture on the Baltimore City Council forever. She was the wife of one of Baltimore's biggest and most colorful business leaders and power brokers, "Little" Willie Adams. Adams was not looked upon favorably although he reinvested his money into the community in the form of shopping centers, gas stations and other kinds of businesses. His wife Victorine had started the very successful program "Woman Power" long before any of those feminist notions became popular. I told Kweisi, "You better watch your back."

Kweisi clearly was the political outsider. When he made the announcement, few thought he had a good chance of winning. He was up against a well established incumbent. The Black voters of the Fourth Councilman District were older and most likely not going to vote for a newcomer, especially someone with an African-like name. But Kweisi had one thing that Victorine didn't have. He had the power of WEAA radio station.

The election was close—a real cliff hanger. Late election night, both candidates were declaring victory. Victorine Adams led Kweisi by a few votes, but no clear majority. Victorine declared victory. Kweisi demanded a recount.

Kweisi got his recount and won his first election by a slim margin.

It was September. I got together with the Goldust Twins, Gerald Bowie and Vernon (the promotion team from Schwartz Brothers) and decided to throw Kweisi an all-out surprise birthday party. In my mind, this party would mark his transition from the world of radio to the world of politics. Gerald and Vernon gave some money, but of course, I did all the work. Since Monday was music day in Baltimore I scheduled the party for a Monday night. I called all the record promoters asking them to chip in. Everybody happily contributed.

One thing about the Baltimore-Washington promoters, we were tight. When it came to getting together to do something, we did it. These were special people, Max Kidd (Independent), Michael Kidd (Atlantic Records), Patrick Spencer (RCA Records), Zeke Zanders (Ariola Records), Gwen Franklin (Casablanca Records), Freddie Richardson (Columbia Records), Barry Terry (Warner Brothers Records), Jimmy Smith (ABC Records), and Susan Perry (Buddha Records). I remember the time we had a formal affair and one of the independent guys wasn't doing well or was down on his luck. One of the guys rented him a tuxedo. It helped to restore his self image, even if it was just for one night.

Everyone came to the table for Kweisi's party. While we were putting it together, there was one sensitive moment for me. We had Kweisi's secretary Doris in on it. On her own initiative she surreptitiously acquired his phonebook and gave it to me. So that was our secret. There was no way we could have gotten a hold of everyone without it. He would know. I was so nervous walking around with his personal phonebook that I broke down and told him. But it was cool. He told me who to invite, and he acted as though it was the surprise of his life.

The element of surprise is not just important to the birthday person, but just as important to the giver of the party. I found out the night of the party, that Kweisi was indeed quite an actor. I suppose this is a talent that he uses quite a bit with his job at the NAACP.

When Kweisi arrived with my girlfriend Renee, he got into the elevator with Don Brooks, the PD at WEBB. Each tried to give the other the impression that they didn't know about it. It was funny. Don Brooks was wondering whether Kweisi knew and tried to play it off as if they were not going to the same place. Kweisi tried to give Don the impression that he didn't know, even though he knew, but he didn't want Don to know that he knew.

Kweisi was overwhelmed by the turnout and the support. Promoters came from Philly, Baltimore and Washington. All the radio people came. The local TV stations were there, and the press showed up, too. It was awesome.

The Road to Nashville

Our regular conference call day at Nashboro was Thursday afternoon. In those days you gave the office a phone number, and the AT&T conference operator called you back at the designated time. This is before all the automated, digital, do-it-yourself, MCI and Sprint technology. On Thursday afternoons I was at my motor vehicle administration job, and I took my conference calls next door at the Mondawmin Travel Agency office, owned by a friend of mine.

I'll never forget that particular Thursday, because Lois, the secretary in the promotions department, came on the phone to tell me that Magruder had left the company. I thought to myself, *Oh no! there goes my great job.* In those days, when the promotion VP left, his whole crew left. The new person always brought in his own people.

Working at Nashboro really was interesting and fun, and I didn't want to lose my job. We had some *really good* gospel product. One thing I learned, which still holds true. When it gets down to the street level, gospel is the blue chip of retail, especially with the "mom & pop" stores. R&B, hip-hop and the rest come and go, but gospel music propelled by its strength, power and conviction just keeps going and going and going. Just look at the history of gospel music and how one generation of pacesetters influences the next. Mahalia Jackson, considered the original Queen of Gospel, and Clara Ward who led the famous Ward Singers to prominence during the golden age of gospel from 1945-1960 laid the groundwork for the success of Shirley Caesar, The Williams Brothers, The Crouches, The Hawkins, and The

Winans. They in turn paved the way for the multi-platinum success of Kirk Franklin. And Kirk Franklin is opening the door for new groups like God's Property and Trin-i-tee 5:7.

I had this sinking feeling as Lois was breaking the news to me. Then she said, "Oh, you don't have anything to worry about—Bud likes you. He just wants to know if you can pull Philadelphia." She was referring to Bud Howell, Nashboro's president and principal owner.

I told Lois, "You go tell Bud Howell that I can sell ice to the Eskimos, and I will deliver Philadelphia." The truth of the matter was, I didn't have a clue about Philadelphia. It was just a place I passed by on the way to New York. But I'd figure it out one way or the other.

Nashboro needed the whole East Coast. The label needed to have the Schwartz Brothers territory sewed up. Schwartz Brothers was their biggest distributor, covering their best markets. They had one problem though. With Magruder gone, they needed me to deliver Philadelphia. I knew that if I could deliver Philly, I would be in a better position to renegotiate my salary.

Bud Howell invited me down to Nashville to talk. As far as I was concerned, the purpose of the trip was to get a raise. After all, I had been working for Nashboro for three years at the same salary. Now I was dealing directly with the president, and they wanted me to cover more territory.

Nashboro was actually quite impressive. They had their own building. Everything was there including a warehouse and recording studios. This was the first time I had actually set foot in a studio, and Nashboro's Woodland Sound Studios was one of the best in Nashville at the time. A lot of other labels recorded there.

Gold and platinum records adorned the walls—The Oakridge Boys, Barbara Mandrell, and Charlie Daniels. MCA, one of the biggest country labels at the time, recorded most of their acts at Woodland. The Nitty Gritty Dirt Band recorded their multiple platinum album, *Will The Circle Be Unbroken,* on the United Artists label there. While I'm seeing all this I'm doing some quick math in my head, and I'm realizing that a ton of money is being made off these records. I'm thinking, *My little raise shouldn't be a problem.*

Bud Howell's office was immaculate, all cherrywood and leather. It looked and felt rich. I immediately liked him. Warm and very, very classy, he had that Southern charm. Since I was born in North Carolina and spent half my childhood there, I knew how to talk with White people from the South. You just speak to them matter-of-factly. You don't come off as a know-it-all, or highly educated, or big-city slick. That turns them off. It was a skill that would pay off for me later. When you're in business for yourself, you have to know who you are talking to and adjust your speech patterns and demeanor to relate to the person, make them feel comfortable and get what you want.

Still I was a little nervous, but I was well prepared. I had notes. I knew everything I had done for Nashboro—radio activity, record sales, and I knew the cost-of-living increase. I didn't waste any time. When I asked him for the raise, he told me how it was a small company in Nashville.

"But I don't live in Nashville. I live in Baltimore where the cost of living has increased tremendously over the last three years," I said.

I got my raise.

Bud told me that I was one of the highest paid people at my level in the company, and he didn't want anyone to know about it inside the company. So to conceal the raise "from the girls in the office," as he put it, he arranged to ship records to Ricky Simone, the gospel buyer at Schwartz Brothers, to cover my increase. It was a nice, neat arrangement. Every month Ricky would issue a chargeback to Nashboro, Bud would ship the product, and I would get my check from Schwartz Brothers. For my chargeback, Ricky didn't order any marginal product, only records that he could sell.

Record business economics—I loved it.

One thing for sure, we always sold records. But to keep selling records, you have to continually come up with new ideas to get exposure for your product. As a matter of fact, we were the only gospel label to have our own radio show. In order to get dedicated air time on the only full-time gospel radio station at the time (WUST in Washington, DC), I came up with the idea of producing our own radio show. The one hour show was produced by the hottest production team in the area, Bobby Bennett (afternoon DJ at WOL, later PD at WOL and then WHUR) and Jack Daniels (WOL production manager). If you ever listened to Black radio on the East Coast, you no doubt heard their production.

Bobby and Jack are the guys that are responsible for all those memorable commercials for live shows. For concert promoters, using Bobby Bennett to do your concert spot is like using Ticketron to sell your tickets. It's just something you *have* to do to sell your show. Their commercial production literally sold hundreds of thousands of tickets. I'm sure if you were to equate their production with ticket sales, you'd be talking millions of dollars.

Well, we applied the same philosophy to our show. We played all Nashboro product and we tagged different stores at every commercial break. The show ran Monday through Friday at 2:00 P.M. on WUST. Schwartz Brothers loved it because it gave them dedicated air time which essentially added up to free advertising for the distributor. They could put out more records, because they could guarantee retailers tags on commercials and airplay. Without spending a dime, they could call up a multiple location retailer like Waxie-Maxie and convince them to take more Nashboro product by telling them, "You'll have exclusive tags on WUST for the next two weeks." Tags are a prerecorded or live voiceover that follow a commercial so the listener knows where they can purchase the product.

The money worked the same way. Schwartz Brothers would issue a chargeback to Nashboro for the monthly production cost of the show. Nashboro would ship the product to Schwartz Brothers, then Schwartz Brothers would cut a check to Bobby and Jack to cover the production costs of the show. What a great system! I loved Schwartz Brothers. Once a month, I'd go to their Wednesday night sales meetings to play new product, go over the status of current releases and bring them up-to-date on future plans.

I was tight with everybody there: Jim Schwartz and his secretary, Rose; Ricky Simone, the gospel buyer; Jerry Jacobs, the sales manager and his secretary, Barbara; Clyde McElvene who ran their Harmony Huts retail division; and even the switchboard operator who later became Mrs. Jim Schwartz.

Anyway, back to Nashville. I'll never forget dinner that night. The whole staff was there—Lois, Billy, Cliff (the promotion guys from the other markets), Shannon Williams (Nashboro's vice president of A&R), and Bud Howell.

The New Orleans Manor, a classic southern restaurant, looked like an old plantation mansion with its white pillars and private dining rooms. It felt very rich, very elegant. It would have been the perfect evening, except we had Steppin Fetchit for a waiter. This guy was from the old school. You could tell that he was used to waiting exclusively on White people. "Yessir boss," was his favorite line, and he would just shuffle along—straight out of *Gone With The Wind*. He might as well have put on blackface and started tap dancing. As a northerner, I was very uncomfortable. As the evening wore on, Bud Howell got drunker and drunker, and the situation got worse—almost abusive. Everybody, including the two promo guys, were just laughing and joking at this guy's antics. I was embarrassed for him, but I guess that's the way life is in the South.

In spite of that one experience, I must say I loved Nashville, and as I look back on it, I couldn't appreciate more having worked for Nashboro Records. Nashboro was so hot, we dominated *Billboard's* gospel chart. The chart would came out once a month, and there were times when Nashboro had 13 chart positions out of 20.

Philadelphia
and the Goldust Twins

With Magruder gone, Bud Howell needed Philadelphia. He needed Philadelphia to solidify the northeast and support Schwartz Brothers ability to pump records out in the Philadelphia market which included Philly, Camden, Wilmington, Trenton, all of Delaware, central and southern Jersey. The Philadelphia territory for Schwartz Brothers was very important. Schwartz Brothers and long-time Philadelphia independent, Universal Records, were embroiled in an intense competition for market share and lines (distribution deals).

I had told Bud Howell in his office that I could deliver Philadelphia. But the truth was, I didn't know *anything* about Philadelphia. I didn't even know how to get there. All I knew is that it was up I-95 somewhere.

Philadelphia was a tough market to break into as a promotion person. In Philly, it was like a family. That outsiders were not allowed to promote records in Philadelphia without going through one of the local promotion people, was the unwritten rule. I don't care who you were, you just couldn't walk into Philly. It just wasn't allowed. So once again I turned to Schwartz Brothers. I immediately called Gerald Bowie and Vernon Thomas (also known as The Goldust Twins), Schwartz Brothers' in-house promotion team. I told Gerald and Vernon I had to work Philly and asked a lot of questions about the market. "Don't worry about a thing, sweetheart; we have an office up there," I was told.

The Philadelphia office was run by Ritchie Salvatore, and the local promotion person was a young man by the name of Waymon Jones. Waymon has since had a very distinguished career, and he is currently the senior vice president of a major label. So the Twins got on the phone, called Ritchie to tell him that one of their manufacturers' reps, Vernice Watson, was coming into Philadelphia and to please have Waymon take good care of her. I was going into Philadelphia on Schwartz Brothers' clout.

The first day I went to work, Philadelphia was great. It was a very pleasant train ride on a wonderful fall day—my favorite time of year. I remember looking out the window and seeing the brilliant fall colors, reds, golds, yellows and browns. I wore a classy, dark green suede pant suit, a hot pink silk blouse from Paraphernalia, with a matching gold, pink and magenta Ellen Tracy scarf and green snake skin boots.

As soon as I closed my eyes to take a nap, the conductor said, "We are now arriving at Philadelphia's Thirtieth Street Station, the only station stop in Philadelphia—Thirtieth Street Station in three minutes."

The station had that classic architecture that you'd see at Union Station in Washington, or Penn Station in Baltimore. Unlike the modernized New York Penn Station, Thirtieth Street Station still had the vaulted ceilings with the long, hanging globe chandeliers. It looked like a 1940's gangster movie. Amid all the hustle and bustle were vendors with carts selling everything from flowers to pretzels to roasted chestnuts.

Amidst all of this quaint charm, comes Waymon Jones. Waymon was an incredibly down-to-earth young man. Although young and innocent, however, he was no kid. Knowledgeable and respectful, he had that "Philadelphia thing" about him. I don't know what it is, maybe because Philadelphia is between North and South or something, but Philadelphia people have this "thing" about them. And I've noticed over the years, that it doesn't go away even when they leave Philly. Maybe it's the cheese steaks.

That was the day that my love affair with Philadelphia radio and retail people started.

The Philly radio and retail people were abrupt like New

Yorkers, but they were friendly like people in the South. Waymon took me everywhere and introduced me to everyone who was important. We went to WDAS and WNAP. We went to King James Records and Webb's Department store. We went to Sounds of Market Street and Smith's One Stop. It seemed like we went everywhere that first day. Between each stop, Waymon gave me the complete 4-1-1 on people I was about to meet.

"Butterball"

Our first stop was the legendary WDAS. I was not sure what I expected, but it didn't look like it sounded. I'd expected a big modern radio station in an office building downtown. Instead it was a building that looked as if it started small and got added onto as they went along. It was at the end of a parking lot somewhere past City Line Avenue which, to me, seemed like the outskirts of the city. But once inside, I realized why WDAS was so successful. Everybody there was like family. The first person I met was Diane Brown. Diane had to be the hardest working woman in radio. She was in the programming department and she was on the air everyday on the AM side which was full-time gospel. In 1980, WDAS was purchased by Sid Small and Eugene Jackson, the owners of the National Black Network. In 1981 they were so enthralled with the success of WDAS AM's full-time gospel format, they purchased WWRL in New York from Riverside Broadcasting and installed the all-gospel format. As the first music director for WWRL's gospel format, Diane commuted from Philadelphia to New York everyday for at least a year. Can you imagine commuting from Philadelphia to New York five days a week? Diane and I got to be good friends, and she and Louise Williams took me under their wing.

The second person Waymon wanted to introduce me to was Joe "Butterball" Tamburro. I had seen his name in the trades and I knew he was a heavy hitter (no pun intended). It just so happens, that day Butterball was not there. So Waymon took me into his office and introduced me to another Philadelphia legend, Buddy Dee. Buddy Dee was the promotions man's promotion man. He was a promoter for WEA (Warner, Elektra & Atlantic Distribution), and he probably taught most of the guys in Philadelphia the ropes. He was kind of like the "elder statesman" among the Philadelphia promo people. Buddy got out of Butterball's chair and told me, "Sit down in the big chair."

They had to coax me because I was naturally a bit apprehensive about sitting in the man's chair. I could just see this huge Black man bursting into the office, finding me in his chair, and my career in Philadelphia would be over before it got started. Well, I was wrong on all counts. First of all Butterball was an extremely nice and gracious gentleman. And second of all, he was White. I was sitting in his chair, spinning around, looking at everything and wondering, *Who is the White guy in all these pictures?*

"That's 'Butter,'" said Waymon. I guessed, unlike in Baltimore, Italians and Blacks were a lot closer in Philadelphia. We don't get along well at all down here. But they seem to do just fine up there. Maybe that's why they call it The City of Brotherly Love.

The Queen and I

If there was anyone other than Butterball who personified what Philadelphia radio was all about, it was Louise Williams. Louise had the early morning shift on the all-gospel WDAS-AM. She was unquestionably the Queen of Gospel Radio in Philadelphia. She had a unique sound among gospel dee jays. She used to do R&B, and she had that polished "sound." She's very attractive, quiet, dignified and deliberate—very well respected. She could be entertaining and political at the same time. On the air she commanded your attention. When Louise talked, Philadelphia listened. Louise Williams didn't just entertain on the air. She taught, and she was controversial. She could talk about last night's concert and a hot political issue in the same breath without missing a beat. She was ba-d-d! *She* had the power.

Louise and I developed a real strong friendship the first year I worked the Philadelphia market. Her birthday was coming up, and I told her as I was leaving the station.

I said to her, "Louise, I'll take you out to lunch for your birthday when I get back."

"Honey, you don't have to do that. Just bring back one of those ba-d-d silk blouses you've been wearing when you come back."

When I went back to Philly, I gave her a lavender blouse made exclusively for Paraphernalia. It was the baddest blouse they had in the store—it was perfect for her. From that point on, we were the best of friends. Our relationship developed to the point that Louise knew me so well, she could read me even if I didn't say a word.

On one trip, after Waymon had accepted a job with Arista Records in New York, I was supposed to be picked up at the train station by the new Schwartz Brothers' promotion person. That day the train was late, and apparently the promo person had left. He actually left me at the train station! Now, I'm a big girl, and I can handle myself. It was no big deal to me. After one hour I called Louise at the radio station to tell her I was late because this guy left me stranded. You would have thought by her reaction that he had left the Mayor stranded. I told her I'd take a cab. She said, "No girl, don't you move, I'll be right there." Louise made a big deal about picking me up. She was actually aggravated because this guy left me. She told several people including Cody Anderson, the general manager of WDAS, what happened. Cody called Ritchie Salvatore and the next thing I know, this guy is calling me to apologize. I bet that was the last time he left *anybody* stranded.

Anyway, Louise pulled up in her brand new Seville and took me to WDAS. She even offered to drive me around to my other appointments.

Around that time, Jim Schwartz had been bragging around the office about how well the Philadelphia operation had been doing. The Twins, Gerald and Vernon, couldn't wait to tell Jim Schwartz, "If the Philadelphia operation is so wonderful, then how come the promo guy left Vernice at the train station? Didn't he even have sense enough to check the schedule?" The Twins really worked that situation. Even though it was a rather insignificant event, any chance to get a friendly "one up" on Jim Schwartz was a chance worth taking.

Just to show you the power that Louise could wield, one day this guy called from Philadelphia and wanted to meet at WEBB radio in Baltimore. He wanted to hire me to promote his record. He was having trouble getting his record played in Philly, a market that was absolutely critical for its success since the artist and the record company were from Philadelphia. I thought it was a little strange that he would come to Baltimore to hire someone to work Philadelphia. But he was paying good money, and I accepted the account.

The first person I called, of course, was Louise. She astounded me when she said, "Give that man his money back. He is a lowlife and you don't want to do business with him. Return his money, and I will replace that account with four more."

I must admit that I was reluctant to give this man his money back. It was during one of those periods when I really needed the money. I gave the money back, and sure enough, Louise came through with four new accounts to replace the one. In this business your greatest asset is your ability to live up to your word—to be there when you say you're going to be there, to do what you say you are going to do, and to deliver what you say you're going to deliver. Louise Williams has all of these qualities. She was *truly* the "queen" of Philadelphia radio.

WEBB'S DEPARTMENT STORE

If you're ever in Philadelphia, find Webb's Department Store. You can tell when you get there because music is blaring outside. Its name is misleading, and it doesn't look like your typical record store. Quite frankly, it's kind of cluttered. There are stacks of records all over the place. It looks like Mr. Webb never threw away a record. What really impressed me—and he still has it today—is an entire wall devoted to singles, 45 rpms. And he does brisk 45 business. It's got to be one of the few places were you can actually buy a 45 rpm of your favorite oldie single.

Mr. Webb is absolutely amazing. He's a dynamo. He can talk to a promoter, answer the phones, deal with the UPS man and wait on customers, all at the same time. Customers, of course, always come first.

Bruce Webb knows the Philadelphia market inside-out. The first day Waymon brought me by the store, Webb stood there and gave me a lecture on the market. He gave me a lecture on the people in the market. He even gave me a lecture on my record company. I learned more about the history of Nashboro Records from Bruce Webb in the half-hour I spent in his store than in all the time I worked there. He told me in great detail all about the people I worked for, their strengths and their shortcomings. He knew if someone at Nashboro didn't follow up on something, or if we had a good record and didn't work it. He had the scoop. Bruce Webb is a true record man. He's probably got vinyl coursing through his veins.

What Goes Around...

Many people helped me along the way—in Philadelphia, Baltimore, Washington and all over the country. But there is one thing that *everybody* told me: "Don't sleep with anybody in this business." Whatever you do at 9 o'clock on the East Coast will be heard on the West Coast by 12:00." I can't say I followed their advice one hundred percent on that particular subject. But I've always been very discreet. And discretion is very important in this business. That's how small this industry is. Your reputation, your word and your credibility is all you have. That's how you attract business, and that's how you make money.

Inevitably, in the record business, the situation will come about when you cross the line from business to personal. By the time 1979 rolled around, I had become a seasoned record promoter. Clayton and I were still friends, but things seemed to be trailing off. I suspected that he had another love interest, but I couldn't prove it, or perhaps I chose to ignore it. What I didn't know was that the gradual decay of our relationship was somehow connected to my inability to get my records played at WOL.

Donna Champion was the music director at WOL, and Bobby Bennett was the program director. Every week I saw Donna. I gave her very nice birthday presents. I took her out to lunch. I did all the right things, but I still could not get my records played. She blamed it on Bobby Bennett, on research, on store reports or the lack thereof—you name it. I got every excuse in the book.

The time eventually came around when Waymon Jones revealed to me what was *really* going on. And this shows just how small the record business is. Apparently Donna Champion, Martin Miller, Clayton, and a niece of Donna's had all been having dinner together when it became apparent that Clayton was having a relationship with Donna's niece. A few of my friends knew that Clayton and I were close friends. So Martin told Waymon and Waymon told me.

When Waymon told me, I hit the ceiling. You never want to hear that someone you really like is messing around with someone else. I got mad, not so much because of Clayton, because I kind of expected something like this, but I was angry because this woman, Donna, had the nerve to block my records over some personal stuff that she really had nothing to do with. Here I was kissing up to her while she was grinning in my face and not playing my records.

I was determined to do two things. Not only was I going to get my records played on WOL, but I was going to get back at Donna. It was no longer business—now it was personal.

The first thing I did was go over Donna Champion's head and took Bobby Bennett to dinner. This was no big deal, because Bobby and I had a working relationship based on the Nashboro radio show. Up until then, I had never talked to him about my R&B records. Bobby said he knew nothing about the situation, and that he would make sure I got a fair shot on my records. Not very long after my dinner meeting, WOL started playing my product.

It wasn't long after that, I got my opportunity for revenge. Cathy Hughes purchased WOL, changed the format to talk, and fired everyone. WOL is now a part of the nine-station Radio One network. When Cathy bought WOL she was ridiculed. Her friends thought she was crazy. How could she take an AM music station that was losing money and market share and make it a success as a talk station? Today, WOL shows a nice profit and is simulcast with WOLB in Baltimore. Donna was forced to pursue a job as a record promoter, which meant she had to come to Baltimore—on my turf!

My office was at the Motor Vehicle Administration at Mondawmin Mall. I was strategically located so that I could get to any radio station within 10 minutes or less. I had gotten some inside information that Donna was about to make her first promotion trip to Baltimore escorted by guess who—Clayton Tucker. It was a Monday of course, record day in Baltimore. This was my chance to show her who was boss in Baltimore. I would never do something like attempt to block her records like she did to me. I just wanted to make a statement. I had a plan. Everything was prearranged.

As soon as Clayton and Donna arrived at WEBB, their first call of day, Sue Woods, the programming department secretary, called me at work. I hustled over to WEBB, walked right past them in the lobby and straight into Don's office where I proceeded to hold her up. This should have struck them as a bit unusual. Clayton always went to his stations early, so I knew I wouldn't be holding up a lot of people. Back to work I went. The next call I got was from Glynice Coleman at WWIN. (Glynice, another dear friend, has since gone on to become a senior vice-president of promotion at EMI Records and is now a thriving independent.) I shot out that door again. Same story, I walked right past them.

On record day, every radio station has a first-come, first-served policy. But on that day, I was a most notable exception. Donna was starting to get the message. I'm sure Clayton wanted to go and stick his head in the sand somewhere. Back to work I went, again. And sure enough, the next call was from WEAA.

By the time I finished making her wait, I'm sure her day was thoroughly ruined. I don't know what happened to Donna, but I don't think her career as a promotion person lasted that long.

For Donna, the moral of this story is, "Don't dish it if you can't take it." For me, the moral of this story is, "Find the right person to kiss up to before you start kissing." As far as WOL was concerned, I was kissing up to the wrong person. By the time I found the right person to kiss up to, Cathy Hughes had bought the station.

THE EMPEROR

If the dee jays were kings, then Jim Schwartz was an emperor. Schwartz Brothers was *the* dominant independent distributor in the Northeast. Schwartz Brothers' primary territory ran from New Jersey down to North Carolina. But just like other independents, they probably shipped records everywhere. They owned the Harmony Hut retail chain too. Schwartz Brothers did very well.

Jim Schwartz and Bud Howell were the best and closest of friends. I never had to go to the airport to pick up Bud Howell, because Jim Schwartz himself would do it. Jim Schwartz and I got along well, but I didn't have that much direct contact with him. It was only in a meeting in Jim Schwartz's office when I saw what kind of man he really was.

In 1979, American Variety International (AVI) purchased Nashboro Records and the Woodland Recording Studios. It was a smart move for AVI. They basically purchased Nashboro for their rich gospel catalog and the Woodland Studios. To this, they added their own established R&B acts. At the time there were larger gospel catalogs out there, but Nashboro had the cream of the crop. It was truly a "blue chip" catalog.

The meeting in the Emperor's office was attended by Jim

Schwartz, Jerry Jacobs, myself, Ray Harris, the new president of AVI/Nashboro, and a guy named Vito who was Ray Harris' hatchet man—in other words, he fired people. I gained even more respect for Jim Schwartz than I'd previously had for him after that day. His main concern was not deal points, or records, or returns—it was people. Jim Schwartz's main concern that day was that his dear friend Bud Howell be allowed to keep his current position and salary, and that the same be done for me. He insisted on those two points, and he got his way.

I never knew that Jim Schwartz had a keen interest in me. What I later found out was that as a direct result of my efforts, Schwartz Brothers' gospel business had increased a great deal during my tenure there. Not only did I promote Nashboro Records, but in the process I taught their sales people, merchandisers, and staff how to market gospel music. This had a direct impact on Jim Schwartz's bottom line, and *that* was his main concern.

Jim Schwartz was loyal. He taught me how really important loyalty was in those days. Today loyalty means very little in the record business. Now you are only as good as your last record. There are no careers any more in the record business—just jobs.

Surprise!

In the fall of 1981, word was starting to get around that I was hired to do national promotion for Word Records in Los Angeles. People were calling me left and right to congratulate me. It was a time in the record business when many of the young, talented and energetic promoters were being tapped for bigger jobs, bigger territories and bigger responsibilities. One day, Zeke Zanders called me to ask if I had any plans for September 19, 1981. I told him, " I don't know. Why?"

"Oh, I thought we could hang out before you make that move to LA," he said.

Now, I don't just hang out. If I have to put on make-up and go out, it better be for a good reason. So I said I would check my calender and call him back. It's not as though my calendar was full, but I was really busy packing to move my life 3,000 miles away. Also I had been in the business long enough to know that I only went places if I needed to be seen—or if I am getting paid. The record business had made me hard like that. I didn't want to become a burn-out, so I carefully picked and chose where and when I did anything or went anywhere.

After he called a few times really urging me to go out, I finally realized that something must be up. Zeke said, "Make sure you are clean." Translation: *Dress up.* So of course I was cleaner than the board of health when I showed up. I wore an off-white suit with off-white satin trim detail on the front of the short style jacket with a matching cream white silk blouse, and, of course, cream shoes and clutch. See, back then I could wear a short jacket and show hips for days. And no hat. Then my hair was black. Now my hair is blond, and I have a hat to match every outfit in three closets—my Sheila Eldridge influence.

Anyway, I drove to Silver Spring, Maryland, and met Zeke at the Holiday Inn. He told me to leave my car and ride with him. I have a thing about leaving my car, so I suggested that I follow him. If I'm not having fun, I thought, I could leave without any problems. I hate that feeling of being stuck somewhere you don't want to be.

As I followed Zeke, I still didn't have a clue where we were going. I thought he said we were going to a dinner and a club. But why was he driving toward Rock Creek Park? Did I misunderstand? Was he picking up someone else? Maybe he said a party.

It was dark, and I was totally lost following Zeke. Maybe I should have left my car. He slowed down and directed me to park. I said to myself out loud, "Oh God, look at these beautiful homes to die for."

Enough is enough already.

I turned to Zeke, "All right! Zeke, what is up? You didn't tell me it was a party. You said dinner, and I'm hungry." Everyone who knows me knows I have a passion for food, and the way to my heart is directly through my stomach.

I was getting a little upset, and Zeke was saying, "Just chill, chill. This will be fun."

We walked up a long driveway to this fabulous house, and there was a security guard there. Zeke said the house belonged to a foreign ambassador. That was an acceptable explanation for the moment. I settled down as the security guard looked at a computer printout for our names. I didn't have a clue. We walked through a gate, and there was this beautiful swimming pool with lights and heaters all around the entire area.

Now this was real strange. I saw (the late) Bill Haywood of Polygram Records, Kweisi Mfume, and Bobby Bennett. And I still didn't have a clue! Then I almost walked into it. A big sign read, *Congratulations!!! Vernice, Freddie, Michael, Patrick and Tony.*

Freddie Richardson, Michael Kidd, Patrick Spencer, Tony Winger and I had all been promoted and were all leaving the Baltimore-Washington market around the same time. I am not bragging, but the cream of the crop of promotion people came out of the Baltimore-Washington market. You had to be a cut above all the other promo people, because this was *the* most important break-out market. You had to go beyond being just regional, and that meant moving to New York, or in my case, Los Angeles.

I must tell you, this was the social event of the year. And you better believe the Baltimore-Washington record promoters did know how to throw a party. It was a who's who, invitation-only party, and I do mean invitation only. I will always cherish the experience as one of the true highlights of my career.

Well, they sent me off in grand style. I didn't know what would be waiting for me on the West Coast—but I was prepared to deal with whatever came my way. Many of my friends and associates had made it in California. I knew I would have to figure out "how the west was won."

A Note of Cooperation

Radio stations compete, but sometimes cooperate on certain issues. A good example was when Teddy Pendergrass was at the peak of his career, he performed in concert on Baltimore's Painters Mill revolving stage. The women in the audience were going crazy for Teddy, and apparently his body guards were being particularly abusive to the female fans with lots of pushing and shoving.

This incensed both Kweisi, Program Director (PD) of WEAA, and Curtis Anderson, who at the time was PD at WWIN. They both pulled all of Teddy's records off their playlist. You could hear them breaking up the records over the air.

GOSPEL MUSIC

INDUSTRY PROFILE

Vernice Watson—Prestige Inc.

By Tim A. Smith

Vernice Watson

When it comes to the advent of promotions, Vernice Watson is recognized as being one of the best in the business.

During her years of professional experience in the area of marketing and promotions, Watson has worked in various capacities. She has served as director of promotions for Lexicon Music; national marketing coordinator for Light Records; account executive for radio station WBGR, Baltimore, MD; assistant general manager, black gospel division, Word Records, and the list goes on.

Like countless others in the world of business, Watson was tired of being an employee and decided to turn the tables and try her hand as an entrepreneur. Thus the beginning of Prestige, Inc.

Inaugurated in 1986, the role of this Pikesville, MD-based company is to, according to Watson, "provide expertise and creative strategies for the development, implementaton and maintenance of promotional and marketing campaigns." Other services the company provides include publicity, public relations and merchandising.

The concept Watson has conceived for Prestige has been successful. During the period from the company's inception to the present, Prestige has been the home base of specialized promotional campaigns for such artists as Aretha Franklin, jazz musician Kirk Whalum, PolyGram/Lection Records, Fixit Records and the cosmetic giant, Revlon, among others.

Is Vernice Watson proud of her accomplishments, especially in a business climate dominated by men? Yes. "My main objective, at the beginning of my career," Watson explains, "was to involve myself with an aggressive, growth-oriented company as a contracted consultant in the areas of advertising, marketing and promotions. After achieving some of those goals, working for other individuals and companies, I decided to do it on my own. I'm glad I took the chance and went the way I did. I have no regrets."

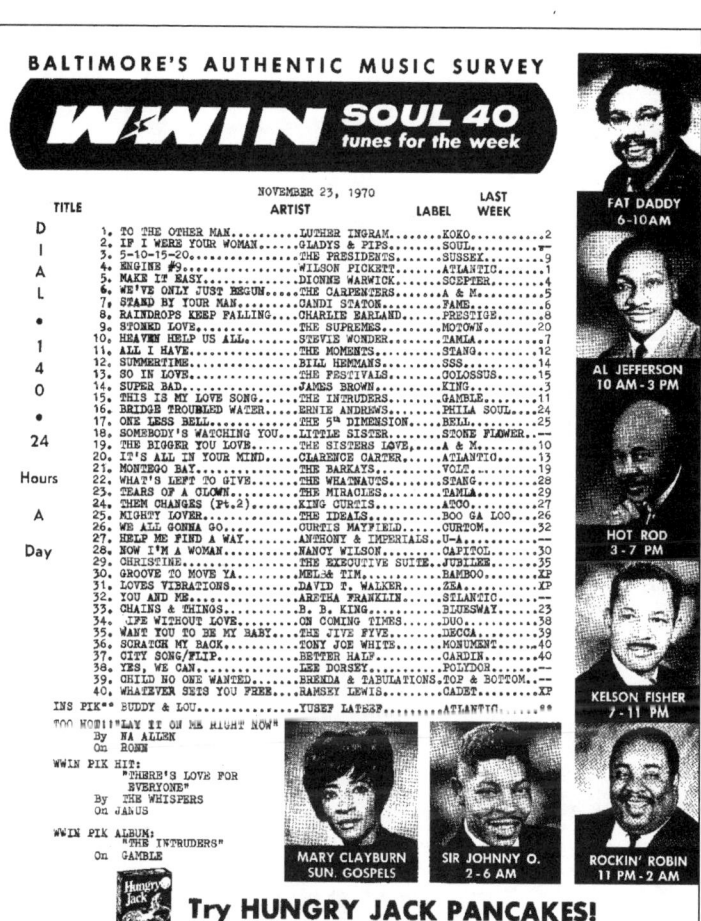

WWIN Playlist. *Courtesy of Ronnie Baker.*

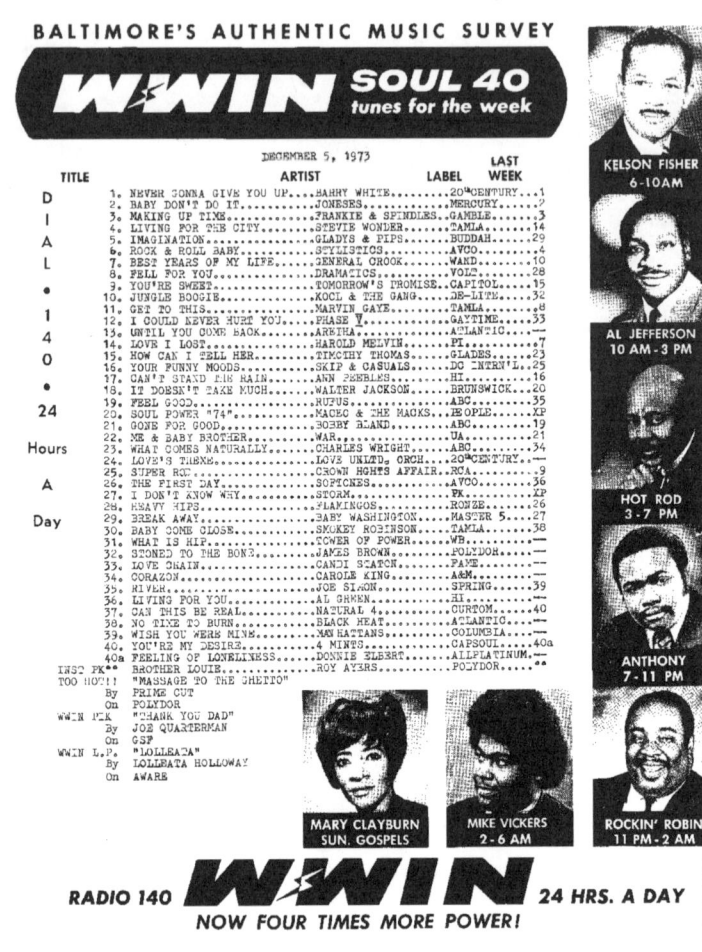

WWIN Playlist. *Courtesy of Ronnie Baker.*

The streetcar that won over Jesse Fax, WHUR's program director. *Photo by Vernice Watson.*

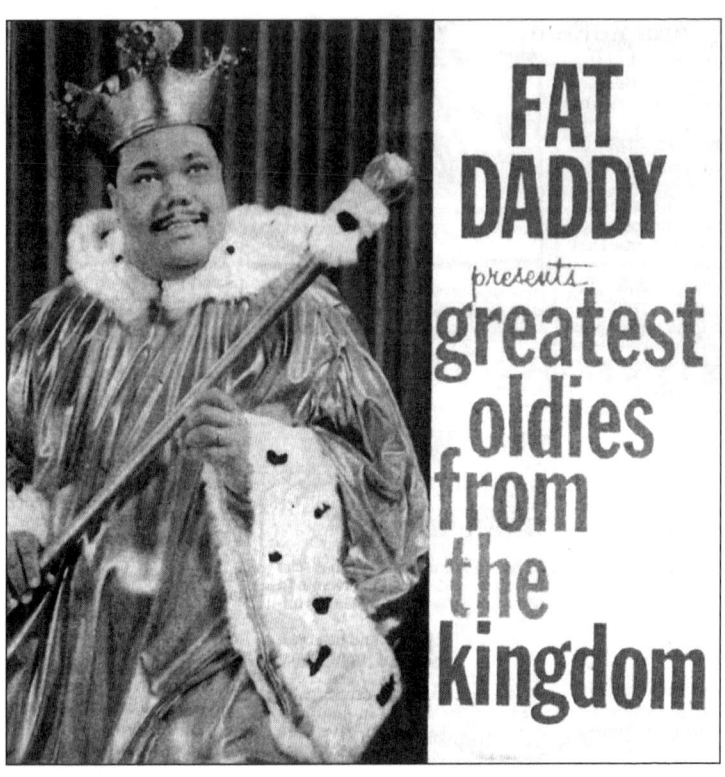

Courtesy of Chess Records.

"Big Al" Jefferson in his office at WWIN, Baltimore. *Photo by Oggi.*

Big Al! A classic pose of "Big Al" Jefferson, program director of WWIN, Baltimore.

Robin Holden, WHUR's top midday personality during the mid-seventies to mid-eighties, now the owner of a major security company in Washington, DC. *Photo by Oggi.*

Vernice with the legendary Joe "Butterball" Tamburro. In an industry where change is constant, Butter has been the program director of WDAS for over 34 years!

Bobby Bennett, "The Mighty Burner," then program director of WOL, Washington. Bobby went on to have a successful run as PD of WHUR and now has one of the most lucrative voiceover and radio production businesses on the East Coast. Also pictured (center), the late Senior VP of Polygram Bill Haywood and independent promoter Max Kidd (right)—taken at the going away party.

Alphie Williams, one of WHUR FM's groundbreaking female DJs. Alphie is now a successful DJ in Oakland California. *Photo by Oggi.*

"Diamond Jim" Sears, General Manager of WEBB, owned at the time by James Brown, with Johnny Guitar Watson. Diamond Jim, a friend of my father's from the old days is now living happily ever after in Southern Florida. Occasionally I see him at a radio convention. Perhaps the most sterling tribute paid to Diamond Jim was during Kwiesi Mfume's inauguration as NAACP head. Kwiesi credited Diamond Jim with being "like a father to me" and credited Jim Sears with "saving me from a life in the streets." Have mercy! *Photo by Oggi.*

Me speaking at my going away party with brothers Mike Kidd and Max Kidd looking on. (Frankly, until recently, I was never comfortable with public speaking.) *Photo by Oggi.*

"The Goldust Twins" The two sinister looking guys on the left are the infamous Goldust Twins, Vernon Thomas (left) and Gerald Bowie. Gerald and Vernon were the indefatigable Schwartz Brothers promotion team during the distributor's heyday. They are pictured with Robert Guillaume during his brief recording career. *Photo by Oggi.*

Jim Henry, VP of Sales for Pearl Records, Vernice and Doug Miller at the Peabody Hotel in Memphis for the 1983 Church of God in Christ (COGIC) Convention. We took Doug Miller's "Joy of the Lord" to #1 on the *Billboard* and *Cashbox* charts at the same time without the support of a "major" label. *Photo courtesy of Jim Henry.*

Vernice's Going Away Party, September 19, 1981. Left to right: Max Kidd (on mic), Patrick Spencer (National Promotion, RCA Records), Michael Kidd (National Field Director of Promotion, Polygram Records), Freddie Richardson (National Promotion Director, East Coast, CBS Records), Vernice (Assistant General Manager, Word Records). Not pictured, Tony Winger. *Photo by Oggi.*

Al Green "doing his thing" at The Modern Music House at Mondawmin Mall in Baltimore. He could have easily won any elective office with his charisma. *Photo by Joseph Wellsey and courtesy of James Bullard.*

Al Green at Modern Music House with the kids. *Photo by Joseph Wellsey and courtesy of James Bullard.*

Al Green with Vernice, Ida Peters *(next to Al)*, Entertainment Editor, Afro American Newspapers and my boss at the time, James Bullard *(next to Ida)*, General Manager, Black Music, World Records. There's that briefcase again!
Photo by Roman Hankewyck and courtesy of Afro American Archives.

Shirley Caesar performing at a Washington, D.C. hotel, 1976. *Photo by Oggi.*

A photo montage from the Verlen Music recording of Trenora Parker and the Los Angeles Cathedral Choir featuring Howard Hewett.

This is a caricature we sent to Michael Powell, a Revlon executive that had inherited the company's professional products division. When we called to follow up, his boss told us Michael was "wrestling the walrus," a reference to the black consumer market.

Ray Parker, Jr. and Raydio join the gang at Schwartz Brothers. Here's a luncheon photo from the heyday of Schwartz Brothers. Some of the key players are pictured (seated, from left) Gerald Bowie (Schwartz Bros.), Susan Perry (Buddah Records), (kneeling) Jerry Jacobs (Schwartz Bros.), (standing, from left) Ricky Simone (Schwartz Bros.), Ray Parker, Jr. & Raydio, (in suit and tie) The Emperor Jim Schwartz, and (on end) Vernon Thomas (Schwartz Bros.).

Vicki Mack Lataillade and me on the road with Deneice Williams at WDAS in Philadelphia.

Vernice and Andrew Young, September 3, 1988.

Vernice Watson named assistant general manager of Word's black gospel division.

Word Announces New Staff Appointments

WACO, Texas—**Vernice Watson** and **Don Felice** have been added to the Word, Inc. family. Watson has been appointed assistant general manager for Word Records/black gospel division, where she will be responsible for artist development. Felice has been selected to hold the newly created position of product manager/Word music.

Vernice with future Congressman and NAACP head, Kwiesi Mfume. Kweisi was Program Director of Morgan State University's WEAA radio station. *Photo by Oggi.*

Nichelle and me during the BRE/Revlon/Cross Colors fashion show that I orchestrated. 1992.

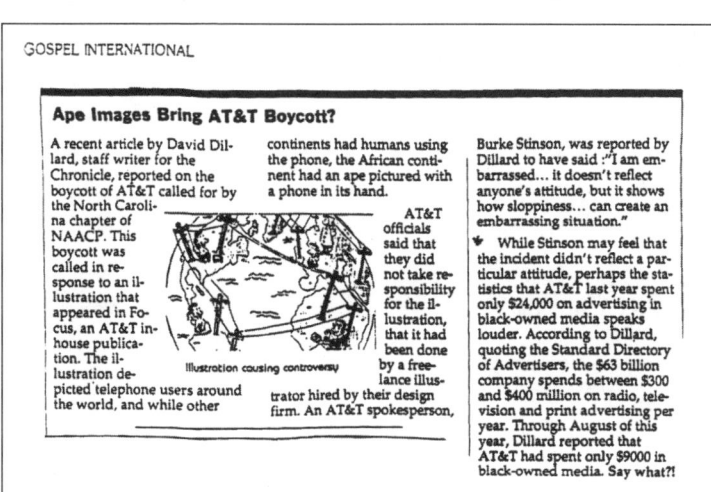

The gorilla.

The MCC Gospel Choir from Minneapolis, one of the groups we distributed through Verlen Music, are an incredibly talented, racially mixed choir headed by Robert "Eddie" Robinson, a virtuoso in his own right. *Photo courtesy of MCC Gospel Choir.*

At the BRE! My client, James Alexander, Vice President, Professional Products Division, Revlon; Columbia Records artist Najee; my daughter Nichelle (isn't she glamorous?) Vernice and Eddie Pugh, Vice President, promotion, Sony Music, 1992

P.O. BOX 2222, NEWBURY PARK, CALIFORNIA 91320 (805) 499-5881

January 28, 1986

To Whom It May Concern:

Vernice Watson has been in the employ of Lexicon/Light since November of 1983. She is a very creative and highly motivated worker. The respect given her throughout the industry has enabled her to do a marvelous job of promoting Lexicon/Light artists.

A very tangible testimony to her ability can be found on the current ballot of the 1986 Grammy Awards under the heading, "Best Soul Gospel Performance By A Duo, Group, Choir or Chorus." Light Records and Lexicon Distribution have all five nominations.

I regret that, due to budgetary restraints and a different strategy regarding promotion, we will not be able to use her services, at least for the time being.

I have personally enjoyed working with her and am happy to call her my friend and can only say she will most certainly make a great addition to the staff of any company.

Sincerely,

LEXICON MUSIC, INC.

Ralph Carmichael
President

RC:lm

   LEXICON MUSIC, INC./ASCAP • LIBRIS MUSIC/BMI • LUMINAR MUSIC/SESAC • CROUCH MUSIC/ASCAP • WALTER HAWKINS MUSIC/BMI • DIXON MUSIC/ASCAP • MAKANUME MUSIC/ASCAP • OOH'S & AH'S MUSIC/BMI • ITS-N-ME MUSIC/ASCAP

January 9, 1982

EXECUTIVES ON THE MOVE

Craft   Watson   Simmons   Payne

Craft Promoted At BIB — BIB Audio/Video Products, Ltd., Hemel Hempstead, England, announced the promotion of Michael Craft to vice president sales, with responsibility for the company's entire United States sales operation. A fifteen year veteran of radio broadcasting and record promotion/marketing, Craft has extensive experience in the music/recording and video industries.
Warner Amex Ups Seibert — Fred Seibert has been promoted to vice president, production and on-air promotion, for Warner Amex Satellite Entertainment Company. Previously Seibert was director, on-air promotion and production. The Movie Channel and MTV: Music Television, overseeing the production of on-air promotion and in-house production for the two services.
Garner Promoted At Endless — Endless Music has announced that Jack Witherby, formerly West Coast promotion director, has now been promoted to the position of vice president of promotion for the company.
Watson Named At Word — Vernice Watson, formerly regional promotion and sales person for Nashboro Records and A.V.I. Records, has been named assistant general manager for Word Records/Black Gospel Division where she will be responsible for artist development, promotion and supervision of the company's field promotion staff.
Changes At Top Billing — Nashville-based booking agency, Top Billing International, has realigned its public relations division appointing Jan Simmons director of creative services, adding Ben Payne as broadcast coordinator and naming Shawn Hagan tour press coordinator. Simmons, who joined Top Billing as national press coordinator last year, will continue representation of Top Billing artists to all print media including the music trades, consumer magazines and syndicated newspaper columnists and additionally will oversee supervision of the division's overall media relationships. Payne, who will serve as both the television and syndicated radio specialist at Top Billing, was most recently associated with Jan Rhees Marketing as sales coordinator. Hagan, who joined the company in the fall of 1979, has been creative services administrative assistant.
Moss Joins RadioRadio — John Moss has joined RadioRadio, the new young-adult network service of CBS Radio, as an account executive based in New York. Moss comes to his new assignment from the West Coast sales office of the CBS Radio Network, where he had been an account executive in the Detroit office of Blair Radio. He also has served with the Radio Advertising Bureau as a national account executive. Moss began his broadcasting career as an account executive with WGCH Greenwich, Conn.
Vestron Names Senk — Susan Senk has been named manager, international marketing for Vestron Video. Senk will be responsible for the implementation of marketing plans for Vestron Video's product release overseas, working closely with Vestron Video's international licensees. She will also oversee all domestic production and media relations. Before joining Vestron, Senk was associate manager creative services at PolyGram Records and at Polydor Records. Prior to Polydor, Senk was international manager/production manager at Lifesong Records.
Fischer And Lucus Taps Jones — Fischer and Lucus, Inc. national record promotion and distribution company, has announced an agreement with John Paul Jones, a nineteen year record veteran, as the company's merchandising director. Jones' background includes six years at Capitol Records, two years with RCA Records and ten years with G.R.T. (General Records and Tapes) as sales manager. His past year has been with an independent label, recently formed Sunbird Records.
Paperny To Gersh — The Richard Gersh Assoc. publicity office has added Janice Paperny

Vernice with the group "Witness" at the annual GMA (Gospel Music Association) in Nashville. In addition to group members, also pictured (standing) Jacque Gibb (Independent Promotion), (second from left); Edwin Hawkins, Raina Bundy (then head of Lexicon, a Polygram Gospel label, now head of Harmony Records, a Sony Red Relativity label.

Vernice with James Bullard during the Word days. *Photo by James Wellsey and courtesy of James Bullard.*

Vernice doing a radio interview in Memphis, 1983. *Photo courtesy of Jim Henry.*

My gorgeous daughter, Nichelle, a model for our client, Revlon, with recording artist Keith Sweat at the Revlon booth during a BRE (Black Radio Exclusive) convention. It was the first time a major hair care company sponsored an event at the BRE.

Chapter 2

Not Just a Job, An Adventure

As I drove across country I knew an adventure awaited me. I finally crossed the state line where I saw a sign that read, "Welcome To California." But deep down I had a sick feeling.

I was giving up two jobs, but I was determined to rise to the occasion. Besides, I had no intentions of staying in California for a long period of time. It was just the next logical step in my career. I was moving into uncharted territory personally and professionally. I decided to go for it. I was going to win.

WORD RECORDS

I had been working as an independent for about a year for Word Records and other labels when Jonas Boston offered me the job as Assistant General Manager, Black Music Division. I was supposed to start in January of '82, but I convinced them to bring me on board in September. I convinced Boston to bring me on four months early, because they were going into the fourth quarter, their biggest period of the year, and they needed the extra help. The Black Division at Word was Jonas Boston, me, his secretary Rockie, and his assistant, "PJ." I had several independents working for me in the field including John Marrs (Chicago), Debbie Smith (New York), and George Scott (Atlanta).

Word was based in Waco, Texas. In fact, Word *was* Waco, Texas. They were the leading company in the inspirational and contemporary gospel market, bringing in millions. Word operated a massive business, the centerpiece of which was their huge sheet music and publishing business. In addition to the corporate offices, the company had a big warehouse and shipping operation. Back then, they were making about $90 million a year!

The Inspirational/Christian Contemporary market was bigger than the Black Gospel market, the foundation of which was a vast network of thousands of Christian bookstores. Word always had a lock on this distribution network, and they pumped their product through it quite efficiently.

When I arrived at Word, the Christian bookstore network sold the top 20 Black gospel records and some catalog but little else in the way of Black product. Distribution of Black gospel product was primarily relegated to Mom and Pop stores, gospel specialty shops like Larry Robinson's God's World in Detroit, and the gospel sections of mainstream record stores.

White inspirational music always outsold gospel, but I was convinced that higher corporate profits were derived from the

Black product. Word, like the other large gospel music companies, spent more money on production and marketing for their White artists but made a higher profit on their Black artists. As a marketing strategy, Word created the Myrrh label to better position their Black gospel product.

Word had Shirley Caesar and Al Green, who were established well enough to fit into their "mass market" distribution system. Black gospel music was new to them. Word saw that companies like Birthright and Light, which for a time were distributed by Word, were selling records and increasing their market share. Word did not want to miss out on a piece of the action.

Word was very established and very Southern. They were not accustomed to marketing Black gospel music in a big way. I never really felt quite comfortable in the role of trailblazer. There was no feeling of permanence or security. I knew I was there on borrowed time. At first, Word did not understand that they needed Black people to get Black records played. They had the machinery to sell, but they needed us on the front line.

Word offices were located in North Hollywood, near beautiful downtown Burbank. We were a new division. You could even tell by how the offices were arranged. We had our place, at the bottom of the Word corporate ladder. Within the office it was as clear as day that there was an "established" side and a side for the "new people." If you walked to the left, you would encounter the "establishment" side which represented the core businesses of music publishing, A & R, and sales. Their offices included flowers, nice furniture, and lush carpeting; we had noisy hardwood floors.

The noise would drive us absolutely crazy as it served as a constant reminder of our differences with the people across the hall.

This division of corporate resources, money and talent affected all of us, even down to the most subtle personnel decisions. For example, "PJ" was assistant to the general manager. She was very talented but, even though she knew the company, did not get the job as assistant general manager. So I explained it to her: "The general manager's assistant is a gofer and a flunky. The Assistant General Manager runs the day to day operations of the Black division."

Perhaps I could have been a little less direct with her. Our relationship was never quite the same after that conversation. The reason she did not get the job was simple and all too familiar; she was the wrong color, White. She never forgave Jonas Boston for not giving her the job and, as a result, was constantly trying to trip me up. But in spite of PJ's antics and in spite of the corporation's lack of knowledge of the Black consumer market, Word was always one of my favorite places to work. The experience of working within a corporate structure and the knowledge I gained has proven to be an invaluable asset to my career.

Barry Terry from Warner Brothers always told me that in the record business, the best situation to be in is when you are in a position that previously did not exist. Then you can mold the job to your lifestyle and have a lot of fun. Maybe this worked for some people, but I was not so sure it was going to work for me. For one thing, this new career "position" that was previously non-existent was only the first of many changes. My living situation went from a four bedroom split-level home in my old neighborhood in Pikesville to a furnished apartment in one of those generic Californian concoctions known as the Oakwood Gardens. This was fine with me, because even though I was going to do my best, I still had my home, my furniture, and my old life back east.

California was simply not my style, and style was something that was always important to me. I admired it in other people, and I enjoyed creating it in myself. Being from the East Coast, I was ready to go to California and do just that.

Soon, however, it became obvious that even being myself would prove difficult. I was not even comfortable at work. I moved to Los Angeles with all these silk dresses, suits and hats. When I went to the office, everyone would come to work dressed in little tennis and jogging outfits or jeans. *Nobody* dressed up. If I dressed, which is what I am accustomed to doing, I felt conspicuous, out of touch and out of place. I had to dress down just to fit in.

I had to face it. I was in culture shock. Where were all the Black people? I missed being around Black people. I wasn't used to this type of segregation. Even Pikesville was half Black and half Jewish. L. A. was a big city but it was divided. It was no surprise when I learned of the Los Angeles race riots of 1992.

I was getting homesick, and I had barely arrived. I felt I needed to get a handle on my situation at home. I was a divorcee and a single mother away from her daughter. I also had a house and a mortgage, and I was used to being in control of my life. My living in California made that impossible. I was not going to gamble away my life—not for Word, not for California, not for anything. There was nothing in California that would cause me to lose everything I had worked so hard for.

But it was not that simple. At Word, I was now an integral part of the Black Music money making machine. So I couldn't just up and leave without serious repercussions to my career—the career that I had worked for so hard and that allowed me to help many Black artists receive the attention they deserved. I had to figure out how I could go home and stay at Word at the same time.

I didn't have a lot of friends when I first moved to California. Sheila Eldridge, who started Orchid Communications, was my best and only friend. Sheila knew Los Angeles well, and she helped me adjust. Sheila, along with Milton Allen, would later help me to play a pivotal role in the development of the Winans, the Crouch's, and The Hawkins' at Light records.

As assistant general manager, I was responsible for the day to day operation of the Black division, including national promotion. I was also in charge of all the independent field people—Debbie Smith, John Marrs, and George Scott. I never went off East Coast time, so I was usually wide awake by 5 A.M. My mornings started out at 7 A.M. with a call from Milton Allen at Arista Records. Barry Terry may have taught me the basics of the business, but Milton taught me how to be a record executive and deal with office politics. He was a product manager at Arista. He understood the inner workings and the politics of record companies. Milton taught me how to go over my agenda, how to handle meetings, field people, and personalities.

I remember him helping me prepare for a big sales meeting. I was taking notes, and I made the mistake of asking him how to spell a particular word. So then he gives me this long lecture on always having a dictionary and always keeping your notes dated in a spiral notebook. From that day on, I usually have a dictionary, and all my notes are kept chronologically in spiral notebooks. (The notes I kept in my notebook formed the basis for my chronology in my AT&T litigation—more about that later.)

I was always the first one in the office. I would get there at 7 A.M. Since eighty percent of promotion work is on the East Coast, even coming in at seven in the morning I was still one hour behind. I'd come in early to reach the programmers who were on the air during morning drive between 6 and 10 A.M. Eastern Time. I stayed late because I didn't really have a life in California. That's really all I did—eat, sleep and breathe gospel music for Word Records. It became my rescuer and my escape.

I shouldn't say I didn't have a life, because my love life did start to get interesting while I was out there. Two friends used to come to visit me. Martin Miller from Philadelphia would come around the time of the BRE (Black Radio Exclusive) convention. He would either arrive a couple of days early, or stay a couple of days afterward. While we had a lot in common and enjoyed each other's company, we were both very busy. He was an East Coast regional promoter, and I was in the process of trying to break Shirley Caesar, Al Green, The Williams Brothers, and The Mighty Clouds of Joy!

Jim, my friend who was a senior executive at General Motors, was another bi-coastal romance. He really liked California, but when he came to the West Coast he came to visit me, not to squeeze me in before or after a business function. He was very romantic. We'd take lovely drives along the legendary Pacific Coast Highway. He'd wine and dine me in the style I was accustomed to—and missed so much.

Then I met Frank. He showed me an even different side of California—not the record business side, but the real business side. I met him at a reception and was introduced to him as the "gospel diva." We both had our own agendas. I was trying to explain to him how gospel music was on the verge of exploding, and he was trying to sweep me off my feet, which he did beautifully.

Frank was the money man behind the promoters. He owned horses, a white Rolls Royce Corniche and was a partner in an investment finance company. I believe it was his influence that inspired me to build my own company. He taught me to think less like an employee and more like an entrepreneur.

When I started seeing Frank, I was in the midst of a divorce, and my credit rating was being trampled. If there's one thing I learned from him, it was the importance of maintaining good credit, because as long as I had credit cards I could finance any project myself without having to go to the banks. At least this was working until I decided to finance an entire live recording and video on my credit cards. Frank helped me get my credit back on track. But it was more than that.

Frank changed my way of thinking, and taught me how to focus on my own dreams. I started to see myself, not as a vice president of someone else's company, but as president of my own company. I had often thought about having my own business. It was difficult, though, to focus on my own business, because I was too preoccupied with what was becoming an increasingly difficult working situation at Word.

I was very militant in my thinking. I always wanted to fight for the artists and the Black division. What I did not understand was that it was not my fight. One day, I was complaining about the politics at Word. Sheila Eldridge gave me some really good advice. She cut me off and said emphatically, "Vernice, if it's not your s——, don't worry about it. Fight for what's yours, what belongs to you. If it's not yours, don't worry about it."

That's why I spent the last five years fighting AT&T. Because that was my business. As I look back on it, one of the most important things I learned from living in Los Angeles was how to be a barracuda.

Nevertheless, it was a challenge working for Jonas Boston. His bosses loved him because he served as a buffer insulating them from the day-to-day pursuit of the Gospel Consumer Market (GCM). He was a natural when it came to representing the company at the NAACP, the Congressional Black Caucus and Gospel Music Workshop of America (GMWA) events. Boston was very easy going, very laid back, a don't-rock-the-boat kind of guy. He carried himself with a lot of class, which was an effective cover for his extreme shrewdness. I was not used to dealing with White people on a corporate level. I had always accepted challenge, but I also learned to fight. California made me tough. It made me grow up.

By the time November of 1981 rolled around, I realized three things. First, there was no autumn in Los Angeles. I missed the beautiful fall colors, and I missed wearing my fall combinations. Second, I was getting homesick, and third—things at home were starting to get out of hand, and I needed to get a handle on the situation.

When I moved to Los Angeles two months prior, I persuaded my ex-husband to move back into the house in Pikesville, to keep up the mortgage and take care of our daughter. I did not want her to leave the Pikesville school system or her friends. I wanted her to stay close to her family and friends and Jones Tabernacle, our church family. I did not want him to mistake this as an invitation for reconciliation, which it wasn't. It was purely a relationship of convenience.

Politics, West Coast Style

After working together for a few months, Jonas Boston knew that he could not handle me. He brought me to Los Angeles because I was the best. I knew my stuff! I was time enough for Boston, Ron Larsen, the vice president of sales, and the rest of them. Although Jonas Boston and I have nothing but mutual admiration and respect for one another today, I'm certain that, then, he saw me as a challenge to deal with and a threat to his new found security. I was corporately naive. Without realizing that I was putting myself in a vulnerable position, I began confiding to Boston, explaining why I needed to go back home. So Boston was telling me that "these people," meaning our senior management, were "Christians" and that I could talk to them about my problems, and they would understand. In reality, he was probably looking for a way to get rid of me. I believe he perceived me as a potential threat to his career. He knew that if I told our bosses I needed to go home, he'd encourage it, and I'd be gone.

Generally, I have found that in the gospel record business,

many executives use the Christian "handle" a little too conveniently for my taste. I've seen individuals pray on conference calls, then turn around and stab someone in the back. I've seen them pump up artists by talking about their music ministry, then turn around and ruin their careers with incompetence. I've seen the worst examples of professed Christian-like behavior right here in the record business. The bottom line is, it's about business, *not* necessarily God's business.

I later found out that everything I told Boston about my personal troubles, he told Ron Larsen. This probably would have been the end of my career at Word except that Ron apparently was able to see my value to the company. In fact, Ron would call the office to speak to the head of publishing—who would quietly give me the phone. Ron would secretly ask my opinion about how things were going and about some of the positions Boston would take on certain matters. Evidently, Ron valued my opinion, and I provided balance for him. They wanted my opinion without challenging Boston's authority. It was their way of checking up on Boston. They would never get rid of him, though, because he was such a good buffer.

Ron Larsen seemed like the kind of person you could not get close to. He was kind of standoffish, blunt and to the point. He was strictly business with a no-nonsense attitude. That was the impression he gave when you first met him. After I got to know him, I found out he was really a nice person. Out of all the people at Word, Ron was the nicest one. I respected him the most. It turned out that he was the one who was really in my corner. That's why I still respect Ron Larsen.

He flew to Los Angeles from Waco, and we went to lunch and

talked about my situation. I was very honest and open. I realized at that moment that I had let my guard down with him, and that put me in a vulnerable position. When it was all said and done, he sent me back to Baltimore for December and January to work the East Coast. I was to meet with Ron and Boston in Atlanta in February to discuss returning to Los Angeles.

    December and January 1982 were two rough months. I realized that in the short time I was away, Baltimore seemed so different. Everything and everybody seemed to move in slow motion. But it was great to be home. It gave me a chance to regroup and try to solidify things. I made sure that by the end of January, everything was back to normal, or as close to normal as it could be. My daughter's attitude toward school had even improved. But her attitude toward me hadn't. She was angry and resentful that I did not take her with me. That was a major mistake, leaving my daughter behind. It is one that I am still paying for today. If I had to do it all over again, that's the one thing I would change. I would have taken Nichelle with me.

    I knew I could only stay in California a little while longer. I needed to be back in Baltimore to move in slow motion. In February I went to Atlanta to meet Ron Larsen, Jonas Boston, and the national sales manager over dinner. That was some meeting. We started out drinking Black Russians, and we never got around to having dinner. It seems as though all we did was laugh at each others' war stories. By the time the night was over, I had agreed to go back to California. I was determined I was going to make it work.

The Big "W"

You had to get a crop duster to fly into Waco when Word used to have sales meetings there. The front of the Word building had a big "W" on it. That "W" had to be two stories tall. I think Word must have been the biggest thing in Waco.

In these national sales meetings, there were about 25 salespeople just drilling you. It was like being interrogated. During one of my first sales meetings, I remember commenting on an Edwin Hawkins record, a Word property, that was absolutely incredible. I kept saying in the meeting that the record was "ba-d-d." Well, they were getting more and more uptight as the meeting wore on. It turns out they thought that "ba-d-d" meant "bad." Fortunately, Gene Whitman, who headed Artist and Repertoire (A&R), the department that signs the artists and produces the music, straightened them out. Gene, who would later become head of A&R at Light Records, was what you would consider to be a "hip" White guy. We literally had to educate Word on the nuances of selling Black music and dealing with Black people.

I remember this one big meeting that everyone came in for. Word's Black business was growing rapidly and represented a nice profit for them. They wanted to learn as much about that part of the business as possible, and they would use these meetings as opportunities to do so. They questioned us (the Black people) at the big meeting in the morning. Then at lunch they rented out a big country club. It was the off season, so no one was there but Word people. Besides Boston, the only Black people present were Hank Mance, Debbie Smith and I. Word had prearranged seating, so there was always one of us per table—and we were grilled individually for lunch.

They even switched tables to make sure they squeezed every available drop of information out of us. But we didn't give them everything. We always met at the hotel at night to decide how much we were—or were not—going to tell them. We controlled the information. Now that was fun!

Perhaps some of the most rewarding time I spent was working with the artists—the Williams Brothers, Al Green, Shirley Caesar, the Mighty Clouds of Joy, the Thompson Community Singers, and the late Milton Brunson. Al Green was clearly the most memorable. Sometimes he took me through some real changes, but he always ended up being a pleasure to work with. There was never a dull moment. Always impeccably dressed, he was very good with people, very personable and down to earth. He had that Southern charm. There was no pretense about him. He was the kind of artist you'd take to Leon's Pig Pen on The Avenue (Pennsylvania Avenue) in Baltimore, or the Florida Avenue Grill on Thirteenth Street and Florida Avenue in Northwest Washington, D.C.

We took Al Green on a promotional tour. Al was wonderful to work with in certain situations, a nightmare in others. You always had to deal with his temperamental personality and his ever-present entourage. There would always be someone there whose specific duty it was to carry his briefcase. He use to say he had his "jewels" in there. In Baltimore, we arranged an in-store appearance at the Modern Music House in Mondawmin Mall. Not one person was in the store except the owner, Steve Garland. I decided that in order to avoid an embarrassing situation and salvage this in-store appearance, I had better round up some people fast.

The limo driver and I walked around the mall while Al Green was in the store with Garland. We told every woman we saw that Al Green was at Modern Music. By the time we got back to the store, it was packed. We could hardly get in the door. It was times like this that Al Green was at his best and was a pleasure to be around. He was a real people person. The ladies loved him. They were all over him, and he was all over them. He was signing autographs, shaking hands and kissing babies. You would have thought he was running for political office. It got so crowded, security had to come in to restore order and set up a line.

Al was great at some things. Then there were times when he was a natural pain in a butt! I booked Al on a local midday TV show on WBAL in Baltimore, hosted by Edith House and Rob Robbins. He was performing live to track. In other words, the microphone was live, but the music was recorded. He was in a playful mood, looking good and feeling good. He was having such a great time, he took off his lavelier microphone and started swinging it around his head like a lariat. The TV studio people were having a fit. It was a live show, so the director couldn't just yell, *Cut!* Al created pure pandemonium in WBAL studios that day. The best I could do was hustle him out of there as soon as he finished. I had to do something to make up for it, because I knew I would never be able to get another artist on their show. So I sent them a plant that was so big it looked like a tree.

Back to Life, Back to Reality

Living in California and trying to maintain my home in Baltimore was taking its toll on me. I was putting myself through a lot of stress. I was having sleepless nights, tossing and turning all the time. Bills were mounting. My credit was in jeopardy. I was going through a divorce. I just knew, in my heart, that I could not stay in California. I was not happy there, but I stayed as long as I could—another six months.

I'd come to the conclusion that it was time to go home. Given the political situation at Word, there was no opportunity for advancement in the company. There was a glass ceiling for Blacks in the industry. For Black women, that glass was a foot thick and armor plated. Jonas Boston was not leaving any time soon. *Where was I to go in the company?* I asked myself. It was time to go.

I had done about as much as I could do for Word. We had several #1 records on *Billboard*. Our product was selling consistently. We were clearly the #1 Black gospel company. We dominated the charts, and we even got several Grammy nominations. I learned what I needed to learn. My job had become less challenging, and my mind was on Baltimore.

I talked to Ron Larsen again. He understood and sent me back to Baltimore with an independent promotion contract with Word Records. I started systematically shipping my things back to Baltimore. Any clothes I was not wearing or anything I was not using I gave away or shipped back. Sheila got all my office stuff, and she was kind enough to help me ship my clothes back East.

This Could Only Be Family

My brother and sister flew to California to help me drive home. I flew them on World Airways which, at the time, could not be beat for the price. It was their first flight. Marnita was cool, but Stanley was nervous.

World Airways was one of those mark-down type airlines, and I was told that they flew into the International terminal. LAX was being rebuilt in preparation for the 1984 Olympics. There was a lot of confusion, and even the people who worked at the airport didn't know what was going on half the time. As it turns out, I was given wrong information. Only international flights arrived at the International terminal. Domestic flights flew into the *Imperial* terminal, which was not on the main airport grounds.

I waited for my little brother and sister at the International terminal, and they waited for me over at the Imperial terminal. Even though Marnita was 19 and Stanley was 22, I still thought of them as my "little" brother and sister. An hour went by, and I started bugging out.

I parked the car, found the World Airways desk, and there was nobody there. It was absolutely deserted—no people, no plane, no nothing. I was getting upset. I called the World Airways customer service number, and they were closed. Now I was *really* upset. Finally, I found someone with some sense who told me where the Imperial terminal was. I drove over there, found the plane, no Marnita and no Stanley. I didn't know it then, but they had gotten on a bus and gone to the main terminal.

When I finally got to the World Airways counter I was furious!

I told them, "My brother and sister are flying for the first time. *Please* help me find them."

It never occurred to me to tell them how old they were. I think they thought Marnita and Stanley were little kids. The airline people did the best they could, but they really could not help me.

Marnita had called me at home, but I had an old style answering machine and couldn't retrieve my messages from outside. This was before voice mail. I just started driving around the airport, and sure enough, after two hours, there they were. I had never been so glad to see those two in my life.

My last stop in Los Angeles was at Sheila Eldridge's house to drop off the rest of my silk dresses for her to ship back to Baltimore. When I got to her house she was not there. I was distraught. I wanted to leave Los Angeles so bad, I just sat there on her steps and started crying.

As luck would have it, Sheila and her boyfriend had just walked up the street for some ice cream, and they hadn't really been gone that long. When she saw that little RX7 two-seater with the three of us all cramped up inside with all that junk, she just shook her head and said, "You know, this could only be family." I hugged Sheila, got on the Interstate 10 Freeway and headed east.

Return Home

The drive was a marathon. I remember waking up at a rest area in Oklahoma somewhere. All I could see were big trucks all around, and there we were in this tiny Mazda RX7. It was pretty intimidating to say the least. We stopped at a restaurant where there were nothing but rednecks. When we walked in, every head turned, forks dropped, and it was as if they had never seen Black people before.

"Don't look at anybody. Pretend you are on the subway in New York; just order your food, and let's get out of here," I whispered to Stanley and Marnita.

We never turned the engine off after that. We just drove—through drenching rain and electrical storms with lightning flashing sideways. I kept calling my dad from the road and he warned me, "Please slow down." But I drove as fast as I could. I didn't know my RX7 could go so fast.

When I got home I did three things. First, I ate my mother's wonderful cooking. Second, I slept for three days. Third, I got a job.

Pearl Records

I began working as national director of promotion for a small Baltimore company called Pearl Records. My relationship with Pearl didn't last very long. But I got two good things out of the deal. That's where I met my good friend Jim Henry, vice president of sales for the label. That's also where I broke the Doug Miller record, *Joy of the Lord*.

I took this record to #1 in *Record World* and *Cashbox* at the same time. This was particularly gratifying, because I didn't have the backing of a major label. It was the first record I had taken to #1 on both charts at the same time, and I got it done myself with good old fashioned hard work. I would later be responsible for Light Records signing Doug Miller.

Relationships are everything in this business. Even though Pearl Records was sold to Atlanta International Records, I maintained the relationship with Doug Miller—and it paid off.

Doug was a good-natured person. A big man, at least 300 pounds with a deep, resonant voice, he was a talented singer and songwriter. Mattie Moss Clark introduced him to the world as a gospel recording artist. Mattie Moss Clark was the mother of the Clark Sisters and, for many years, the Minister of Music for the entire Church Of God In Christ (C.O.G.I.C.) organization.

Although Doug was very big in size, he was also very humble. He always had the utmost respect for Mattie Moss Clark.

I'll never forget the time I was attending the C.O.G.I.C convention in Memphis with Doug and my close personal friend, Pearl Records Vice President Jim Henry. We stayed at the Peabody Hotel in Memphis.

The Peabody is a classy Memphis institution known for the "Peabody Ducks." Everyday at 11:00 A.M. and 5:00 P.M., these ducks march out on a red carpet, one by one, in a straight line, directly to a fountain in the middle of the lobby. The hotel makes a big deal out of it. There's music, a "duck master," and a big introduction: "Ladies and gentlemen, introducing an institution for umpteen years, the Peabody Ducks." Kids crowd around. People take pictures. It's an event. Those ducks probably live better than most people. When they're not in the fountain, they are in their "penthouse suite." Whenever you're in Memphis, you have got to see these ducks. It's a Memphis thing.

Anyway, we were on the Peabody parking lot, and we had just

gotten out of Doug's Rolls Royce. It was the first day of the convention, and the hotel was packed with C.O.G.I.C. people, ministers, choirs, everybody. The valet who got Doug's car revved up the engine like a racing car, then backed out really fast and hit another car. Doug lost it. He yelled an expletive at this young man so loudly that everything literally stopped. Every car stopped, every head turned. I'd never heard anyone yell that loud in my life. He yelled so loud, and his voice was so deep, you could almost feel it going through you. I think that valet was probably shaken for life.

Like so many small gospel labels, Pearl came and went. But it was still a rewarding experience for me. Unlike Word, where I worked established artists like the Mighty Clouds or Shirley Caesar, Pearl gave me the opportunity to break a new artist and take the record to #1. There's nothing like the feeling of knowing that through your own hard work, for that one week, you have achieved something no one else has. I was number one! I was able to use the tools and the national contacts I developed at Word to make it happen. After Pearl, I still had some independent accounts, but I needed the steady income a job would bring. So I turned to radio.

I was still in good with Baltimore radio. Everything in those days was clout. It was who you knew. I called everyone I knew in radio to let them know I was back in town, and I was looking. My good friend, Lou Hankins was on the air at WAYE (now WBGR), a full-time gospel station. Vashti McKenzie was the general manager. Lou told me the station had an opening in sales and had spoken to Vashti on my behalf. I told Vashti in the interview I could sell anything, and she hired me on the spot. Working at the station helped me get reestablished in Baltimore, and I cemented some lasting friendships.

My very first ad came from a law firm right up the street from the radio station. I walked into the law office cold, found out who was responsible for spending the money at the firm, gave my pitch and got my first account. The man who held the purse strings for the firm was Vernon Simms. He and I have been good friends ever since. Vernon went on to become Kweisi Mfume's campaign manager and now works on the staff of Congressman Elijah Cummings. Vernon would later play a key role in my entree to AT&T.

WAYE also put me back in contact with my best friend from high school, Jean Alston. Jean was a weekend announcer on WAYE, and she saw my name on a mailbox in the office; that's how we got back together. Jean was always very aggressive. When we were in high school, another girl wrote the "B" word in my slang book. A slang book is a regular composition notebook that is devoted to things other than academic pursuits, or, for lack of a better term, "slang." Several pages are devoted to your girlfriends. I had a page, Jean had a page, and so on. The book would get passed around the school for people to sign. It was a keepsake. When Jean found out about what that girl wrote on my page, she wore her out. I'm sure that girl wished she had never met me or my slang page. That's how we got to be such good friends.

Jean told me she wanted to get in the record business, so I took her to all the radio stations, showed her what to do, where to go and how to do it. I trained her as a promotion person. I did the same thing for her that Barry Terry from Warner Brothers did for me. Jean became one of the more successful independent promoters in the area, with at least fifteen gold and platinum records to her credit. Now she's enjoying life as the nighttime personality on a 100,000 watt FM full-time gospel station in Montgomery, Alabama.

I also met April Washington, another account executive at WAYE. I trained April as well, and she has gone on to work for major labels like RCA, EMI and Motown. She is now doing very well with her own promotion and marketing company.

One thing Frank always said, "No matter how much you get paid when you work for someone else, or what kind of position you have, you still have to answer to someone—and you can still be fired. You can always get a job, but the way to really make it in this business is to have your own."

Neither Jean nor April have ever looked back.

Light Records

While I was working at WAYE, I got a call from Robert Hankins, an independent promoter from Detroit with whom I worked at Word. He was a White guy who worked the Christian and inspirational market for Light Records, and he didn't have a clue about the Black gospel market. He had asked around and got my number from a few radio people. One thing about the record business. It is so important that you conduct yourself professionally and that your word is good. When you are an independent, all you have is your reputation. Nothing is more important. Your reputation is your lifeline in this business.

He hired me to promote the album *Sandra Crouch and Friends* in the mid-Atlantic region. I hadn't heard of Sandra Crouch or her music. I figured she must be related to Andrae Crouch. Somewhere along the line I found out that Sandra was Andrae's twin sister. The *Sandra Crouch and Friends* album was ba-d-d. It had an awesome track, *Holy Spirit*. The song had wonderful lead vocals. Sandra was not the greatest singer, but she was a great songwriter and stylist.

Hankins told me that Sandra was coming to town, and the label wanted me to set up the promotional tour in the area. I started prepping the market. I put together a promotional campaign for Baltimore, Washington and Philadelphia that I doubt Ms. Crouch will ever forget.

Sandra didn't know what to expect from a promotional tour of the East Coast. I worked Sandra Crouch. And I mean I worked her! She had never worked like this before. I took her everywhere, from radio stations to retail stores, from television stations to the Shake & Bake Roller Skating Rink on Pennsylvania Avenue in Baltimore.

Known as "The Avenue," Pennsylvania Avenue is the historic mecca of Black Baltimore. In the 50's, it was the heart of Black Baltimore night life. The world famous Royal Theater, which for decades showcased the best in Black entertainment from Moms Mabley to James Brown to the Five Blind Boys and the Swanee Quintet, was located there. On Easter Sunday there was always a parade down the Avenue. People would wear their best clothes and there were bumper-to-bumper Cadillacs polished to a "T."

If you ever have an artist who has an ego problem and

requires a little humbling, make your first stop, preferably breakfast, in the heart of the ghetto. You've been there before. It's the place with the neon sign and the fresh pastries in the window. The owner is sitting behind the cash register, and there are dusty autographed pictures of celebrities who once dined there. Usually that experience will straighten out an artist's ego fast.

I borrowed my ex-husband's Seville and drove Sandra Crouch all over three states. We made all the right contacts. Sandra was very demanding. She wanted results. And she got them from me.

We went to every radio station—WWIN, WEBB, WSID, WEAA and WAYE in Baltimore. We went to WOL, WHUR, WUST and WOOK in Washington, D.C. We even went to Annapolis to see "Hoppy" Adams at WANN. We used every available moment of the day, taking every opportunity to spend quality time with radio people. Breakfast, lunch and dinner always included someone who was important in the market.

When we completed the promo tour, I put Sandra on the train for New York. She was absolutely exhausted but happy with what we'd done, because I ended up breaking her record out of the mid-Atlantic region largely based on the promotional work we did together. She was able to see directly the results of my efforts and hard work.

I called Debbie Smith in New York for her to work the New York leg of Sandra's promo tour. I warned Debbie that Sandra was demanding and to make sure that everything was set up properly. Evidently, Debbie didn't heed my warning and I got a constant barrage of phone calls from both of them complaining about each other.

The situation, however, turned out to be a blessing in disguise.

Not to take anything away from Debbie, but the difference between her style and mine was apparent to Sandra. At the time I broke Sandra's record, her brother Andrae was in the midst of renegotiating his contract with Light. He was represented by agent Ramon Hervey (who eventually married his biggest client, Vanessa Williams). Sandra convinced Andrae to make sure that as part of his deal, Light Records would hire me as their National Director of Marketing. To put the icing on the cake, I ended up taking Sandra's record to #1 on *Billboard!*

During that time, Light Records was on the verge of bankruptcy. It had been a long time since the days of Gentry McCrary when Light was able to put a consistent marketing effort behind a Black gospel release. Light had been an on-again-off-again powerhouse in Black gospel. One man was responsible for both states of being. That man *was* Gentry McCrary.

KING OF THE HILL

Light Record's big artist throughout the 70's was Andrae Crouch. Gentry McCrary, a veteran gospel promoter, was handling the Black gospel roster. From 1974 to 1981, he did it all—A&R, promotion, sales, whatever. Gentry made a lot of money for Roger Carlyle. I always had a great deal of respect for him. He's someone I looked up to as the first Black gospel music executive. He was the first, and for a while, the only Black person hired by Word records in 1971 as their director of national radio promotions. He was a trailblazer. He was "King of The Hill."

The myth is always bigger than the man. Gentry had gotten

a Mercedes Benz from the company, and it was a big deal to those of us on the outside looking in. Senior level Black record executives working at the majors got fancy cars, but at that time it was unheard of in the gospel world. Maybe some of the big White sales guys got Mercedes, but certainly not anyone Black. Gentry even convinced Roger Carlyle to give him his own label.

Carlyle, grateful for Gentry's tenacity in selling product which kept Light Records alive, reactivated his old Luminar label for his "director of national promotion" to do with as he pleased. Gentry was able to sign artists—another first! He got Roger Carlyle to give him a brand new Mercedes and his own label.

When I talked to Gentry about all this, he played it down. He said the car was no big deal, that it was from his car allowance, and he was smart enough to figure out how to get a *used* Mercedes for that price. As far as the label was concerned, Gentry said he convinced Ralph to let him have his own label to pick up existing master recordings. I told Gentry, when I spoke with him recently, "The real facts don't count." What he did at Light was truly an inspiration for all of us who were aspiring to make something great happen in gospel music.

The marriage with Gentry and Carlyle was over not long after Gentry got the Mercedes. Benson Records, a gospel powerhouse out of Nashville, sought Gentry out. Everyone in the industry knew of him. The fact that he was developing a label at Light Records, caught Benson's attention. They offered him a two-year contract to develop a new Black gospel label. In 1981, the same year I went to Word, Gentry cut a deal with Benson, packed up the Mercedes and drove to Nashville.

But he took more from Light than that Mercedes. He also

took the artists he had been considering for his Luminar label, most notably, Vanessa Bell-Armstrong. Gentry started the Onyx label for Benson and had a number one record with *Peace Be Still* by Vanessa Bell-Armstrong. He also signed Thomas Whitfield, The Richard Smallwood Singers, Janice Skinner, and Freddie Stewart (brother of Sly Stone). The point is, Gentry played a major role in building up two labels into Black gospel powerhouses.

An epilogue on Gentry's story: The relationship with Gentry soured at Benson, and Gentry left at the conclusion of his two-year contract. But this time there were no artists to take with him and no shortage of qualified Blacks to replace him. I am told that he had a stroke and a few bad years following the debacle at Benson. Now he's back in the business and is starting his own label. God bless Gentry McCrary. He's a man worth being called, "King Of The Hill."

Roger Carlyle

Vernice Watson is a very creative and highly motivated worker. The respect given her throughout the industry has enabled her to do a marvelous job of promoting Lexicon/Light artists.

A very tangible testimony to her ability can be found on the current ballot of the 1986 Grammy Awards under the heading, 'Best Soul Gospel Performance By a Duo, Group, Choir or Chorus.' Light Records and Lexicon Distribution have all five nominations.

Roger Carlyle

Roger Carlyle gave the appearance of a gentle, kind and trusting man. He was a businessman who liked making records. A recording artist and song writer in his own right, he had been making money in the Inspirational/Christian market for years. As an artist, Carlyle reminds me of one of those late night commercials where you never heard of the guy, and you see him playing the piano with the song titles crawling up the screen. He was a very distinguished looking gentleman with a mane of white hair and very distinct features.

Earning and losing most of his money from music publishing and horse breeding, Carlyle earned and lost millions. Like Word, he was attracted to the profits that Black gospel could bring. But I don't believe Roger Carlyle was ever prepared to deal with the volatile personalities of Black people in the music industry. He trusted Gentry McCrary and practically lost his entire Black artist roster. He was lambasted publicly by Andrae Crouch. He was threatened with bodily harm by the manager of one of their best-selling groups, and he was taken to the bank by John Marrs and his cronies.

Poor Mr. Carlyle. He finally ended up selling Light Records. But more importantly, he lost so much money with the record company that he sold his Lexicon Music catalog, one of the most lucrative gospel/inspirational publishing catalogs and a major source of his wealth.

True Colors

Roger Carlyle was an affable White man, but he showed his true colors to me when we were at the NARB (National Association of Religious Broadcasters) convention.

They wanted me to take one of their White artists around the convention to meet people. I knew it was a stupid idea, so I came up with an alternative. I ran into a friend from Baltimore, Carroll Johnson, who had a small label, and I made a deal with him to share his booth space on the exhibit floor. It was a good arrangement, because Light was now on the convention floor, and Carroll's little company had a better profile. (Years later, Carroll's son, Duane, would become the program director for Gospel Grace, one of the most influential Sunday gospel radio programs, WEAA Baltimore, Morgan State University's station. Duane's current gospel show on Radio One's WERQ-FM, (92Q) is the number one-rated show on the entire urban-formatted station.)

The booth was a big hit, and it attracted a lot of people. I finally got a chance to introduce Roger Carlyle to Carroll. No sooner than I had said, "Mr. Carlyle, I'd like you to meet the man who is responsible for us getting our booth space," Pat Boone walked toward us, and Carlyle caught his eye. Carroll and I were excited because we assumed we were going to meet Pat Boone. Without saying *excuse me* or *just a minute*, Roger Carlyle turned his back directly to us to greet the singer. He took four giant steps away from us, then proceeded to walk away without so much as batting an eye.

That's when I knew how I stood with Roger Carlyle. More importantly, I saw how Black people stood with Roger Carlyle.

Breathing New Life Into Light Records

When I joined Light Records, it was a bankrupt company. Mr. Carlyle had filed for protection from his creditors. I knew they would try to use this as a negotiating point, to try to convince me to take a less than desirable salary. The deal I cut with them was simple. I knew from my previous experience in Los Angeles that I was not about to move back there. I agreed to run their national promotion as long I could work out of Baltimore. I told them, "If you can't pay me top dollar, you surely don't expect me to move to Los Angeles."

The truth is, I was very happy with what they agreed to pay me. Here's my golden rule on negotiating: Always ask for more than you expect to get, and always offer less than you're willing to pay. In this case it worked perfectly. I asked for far more than I knew they would be willing to pay, and as a result, they were more than willing to have me based in Baltimore as a compromise.

The bottom line here was I still got what I wanted—a decent salary and I got to stay home.

I was willing to go on the road, go to Los Angeles for meetings and attend conventions. I would even spend some time in the Burbank office. But I was not moving back to Los Angeles.

It was in the Burbank office of Light Records where I met another long time friend, Jacque Gibb. Jacque was their promotion manager for the Christian contemporary market. Jacque now has her own company, AM-FM Promotions, and is one of the most successful independents in the Christian contemporary market. Since then we have collaborated on scores of projects ranging from Motown to The Sounds Of Blackness to Mariah Carey on Sony Music.

At Light I had a lot more latitude than I did at Word. I wasn't just calling radio stations, I was getting involved in the planning of releases, marketing strategies and artist development. Light hired a novice named Jay Franklin as a "vice president of marketing." He didn't know anything about marketing records. The rumor mill had it that his relationship with Light's Vice President of Artists and Repertoire, Jean Whitman, was *more* than casual. He had a lot of energy and *one* good idea.

Jay came up with the slogan, "Light Records...The Artists' Company." The whole concept behind the slogan was that Roger Carlyle was an artist in his own right, and that the label supported its talent through artist development. I looked at this as a challenge, because we now had to stand behind our slogan.

One thing I liked about my job at Light was it gave me a chance to be innovative. I worked hard to create new and different promotions to support the artists. Since money was tight, I often went to the artists themselves or their managers to contribute to this effort.

The Lexicon Music sales staff was far removed from the creative process. We had all these telemarketers and sales people who had no real emotional connection with the product. They just sold titles and stock numbers. I wanted to get the sales department solidly behind the new Andrae Crouch project—our most popular artist. I went to Andrae's manager, David Del Sesto, and we came up with the idea of having a poolside cookout and performance for the sales people at Andrae Crouch's home.

It was the perfect situation. I brought the salespeople together with Andrae, and I didn't have to pay for it. All the Light salespeople were there including all their telemarketers. And what a cookout it was!

There was an impromptu performance with Andrae playing his grand piano and Tata Vega singing selections from Andre's new album, *No Time to Lose*. Andrae even gave out a $500 door prize. This was a very effective activity. As a direct result of the cookout, we pre-sold 60,000 units!

All this Black music was being sold, but as is the case in most record companies, all the salespeople were White and male. There was only one Black telemarketer there, a young man by the name of Alfred Liggins who was attending UCLA. His mother is Cathy Hughes, the owner and CEO of Radio One, the Baltimore based chain of radio stations. Alfred is now the President of Radio One, the largest Black owned and operated radio chain in the country.

Building The Team

The next thing I did was hire Orchid Communications, the company owned by Sheila Eldridge. Milton worked with Sheila as her general manager, and Jalila Larsuel was a publicist. This worked out since Orchid was right there in Hollywood, and they became sort of an extension of me. They could be in Jay Franklin's face all the time. That would take some of that pressure off of me. I knew Milton could handle Jay Franklin. Jay needed a tutor and Milton was perfect for the job. It turns out that Orchid's involvement, along with the new things I was doing with the artists, helped lay the groundwork for gospel to truly crossover into mainstream R&B.

Enter Vicki Mack.

Milton and Jalila called me one day to suggest that I hire this young lady, Vicki Mack, as a merchandiser. Her job would be to go around to record stores in Los Angeles to promote and merchandise the product. The first time I talked to her on the phone, I was thoroughly impressed with her market knowledge. The Los Angeles market was not like the East Coast. The gospel radio programs did not effectively cover the market.

Vicki explained that in Los Angeles, most gospel music sold on the strength of word of mouth. Therefore point-of-purchase and merchandising the product would be key to developing sales. Merchandising had been going on in an organized fashion in the record business since the mid-seventies, but it was new for gospel music. We needed Vicki to complete the "TEAM," plus I owed Jalila a favor for keeping my black sports car in her garage in Pasadena while I was on the East Coast working those two months for Word. I hired Vicki right away.

Vicki's first job in the record business was at RCA records as a merchandiser. Gentry McCrary then brought her in at Light for a short time as an intern. She is now the CEO of Gospo-Centric, and her husband, Claude, is the CEO of B-Rite Records, the two leading independent gospel music companies today. Vicki and Claude started their first company, Charismata, around 1984 with one computer and an idea to apply contemporary marketing techniques to gospel music. Vicki is someone who is truly living her dream. Today their releases dominate gospel music sales. Her artist, Kirk Franklin, has led the most profitable tour of any gospel artist in history. She has a very lucrative publishing company that includes Kirk Franklin and God's Property and other major artists. Vicki's distribution is now with Interscope Records.

I told Vicki, "I'm not jealous of your #1 record, but I'm envious because you get to pass *John McClain* in the hallway."

It would be almost another 10 years before gospel music would gain mass acceptance on R&B radio, but the groundwork was laid right there at Light records in 1984. All that talent, energy and drive came together on the Winans' *Tomorrow* album.

THE MAKING OF A MOVEMENT

Tomorrow was the third release on Light Records by a family of four brothers from Detroit. *Tomorrow* represented more than just breaking a record, it started something big—something really big. It represented a key building block in contemporary gospel's movement. It represented contemporary gospel's move from obscurity to mainstream and, ultimately, to R&B radio. In the mid 80s, the vast majority of gospel radio stations focused on more traditional forms of gospel—quartets, choirs and the like.

"Contemporary" gospel, or gospel with elements of R&B, did not get as much airplay and was often relegated to some obscure rotation category on gospel radio play lists. There had been breakthroughs before with Edwin Hawkins's *Oh Happy Day,* Andrae Crouch's *I'll Be Thinking of You,* and The Clark Sisters' *You Brought the Sunshine.* But the Winans were truly the first group to break through in a major way where all their subsequent releases received mass acceptance. Now "Winans" is a household name that is synonymous with record sales.

Everybody from Mom and Pop Winans on down are making music and doing very well at it. And it all started at Light Records in 1985 with *Tomorrow*. Breaking the Winans was a collaborative effort between the record company, the Winans' management, and the public relations firm that I orchestrated.

We did a full court press on the Winans. When they came to Los Angeles, we treated them like a major crossover act. Not only did we do gospel radio, we went to R&B radio, Orchid set up a press luncheon, and Vicki set up in-stores. We visited mom & pop stores, churches and community centers. We did television appearances and autograph signings.

As the record began to soar, Aaron Glenn, the Winan's manager, pulled together a major-market concert tour. The strategy was to put the Winans in classy venues more associated with mainstream acts than typical gospel quartets. Venues such as the Fox in Atlanta, the Beverly in Los Angeles or the Sanger in New Orleans played host to the Winans tour. We rallied around each venue with retail merchandising, radio promotions, advertising and sales promotion. We pulled out all the stops. Soon the industry buzz was that the Winans show was *the* show to see.

I was very specific on what I wanted to happen on this campaign. I told Milton, Sheila, Jalila and Vicki, "The Winans must get the same treatment and be handled the same way that any major R&B act would be handled. Everything has to be first class. There will be no secondary treatment because this is a gospel group!" The team pulled through in flying colors. Ours was the first real "A-Team!" My strategy paid off in record sales and concert tickets, and the Winans never looked back.

Bringing *Tomorrow* to #1 had a major impact on Light Records. It actually became a pleasure to read the weekly sales reports, something I had always dreaded. I began to look forward to watching sales figures increase every week. I could actually see the fruits of my labor on paper. For the moment, the success was great for the label. But success in the record business is a double-edged sword. The Winans were still operating under the original contract negotiated by their first manager, Derek Dirkson. Without the foundation Derek laid for the Winans, the successes we were enjoying could never have been realized.

The success of the Winans put Aaron Glenn in a very strong bargaining position with Light. He demanded an immediate renegotiation of their contract. Aaron had other plans for the Winans. His mission was to take the Winans mainstream—and what we did at Light gave him the springboard to do it. Aaron was going to do whatever he had to to get out of that Light contract. Even if Roger Carlyle were to agree to his terms, Aaron didn't believe that Light, a gospel label, could take the Winans where he wanted them to go.

First he demanded outrageous terms that he knew Roger Carlyle could not meet. Then he threatened to withhold Vanessa Bell-Armstrong, another one of his artists that was signed to Light from the label. Roger Carlyle really had no obligation to renegotiate their deal. He already had a deal.

Finally Aaron just used some good old fashioned Detroit coercion—he threatened. It turns out that Marvin Winans had written a song for Light's new artist, Howard Smith, which was ready for release. For whatever reason, there was no songwriter's agreement for Marvin's song. Aaron knew it and threatened to hold up the Howard Smith album indefinitely. He was well within his rights to do so, because a simple songwriters agreement with Marvin Winans had not been executed, and the record had already been manufactured. That was a little more than Mr. Carlyle could stand. Not long after that, Aaron had his release.

The next Winans album was on Quincy Jones' Qwest label. It got the backing of the entire Warner Brothers and WEA marketing machine. But more on the Winans and Warners later.

Prime Time at the BRE

By the summer of 1985, Light Records was on fire. The Winans record was still selling through, and I had negotiated the deal to sign Doug Miller. The Sandra Crouch and the Walter Hawkins records were doing well, too. Light even signed two new artists, Howard Smith and Debbie McClendon, the wife of producer Scott Smith. I think by that time we felt we could break anything.

The Black Radio Exclusive (BRE) convention, the major gathering for the Black music industry, was coming up in Los Angeles, and I was not going to let it pass by without making some kind of major statement.

I flew out to Los Angeles and convinced Light to back me on doing a major presentation for the conference. Until then, gospel had always been put off until a Sunday morning breakfast and panel when virtually everyone was sleeping. After I got the label's backing, I went in to negotiate the deal with BRE's publisher, Sidney Miller.

We wanted a prime time slot and were willing to pay for it. For the first time that I am aware of in the history of Black music conventions, gospel music hit BRE prime time. We negotiated a Saturday afternoon luncheon and showcase to be followed by a gospel panel. That luncheon changed many of the limiting preconceived notions that programmers held about gospel music. It was a first class event that I produced with the help of our A-team. Vicki did an outstanding job of merchandising that room. She completely transformed it. Orchid helped me promote the event and get all the right people there.

Walter Hawkins and Doug Miller performed, and in another first, we debuted the Winans music video during the luncheon. The fact that the Winans even *had* a music video was in itself unique. Gospel artists did not have promotional music videos in 1985. Don Allen, then program director of WWRL in New York, the hottest gospel station in New York, was the M.C.

The panel followed with Gene Whitman, Jay Franklin, Don Allen, and yours truly as moderator. Perhaps the most significant thing about the panel, though, is I invited Vanessa Vaughn from the nationally syndicated gospel show, Inspirations Across America. Vannessa, now with the new Sheridan Gospel Network, recently told me she considered that panel as her first major national introduction to the record business.

That BRE changed the way a lot of programmers perceived Gospel music in relation to their own formats. After the luncheon, I got a call from Al Hobbs, general manager of WTLC in Indianapolis, a mainstream R&B station. His program director at the time, Jay Johnson, was so impressed by Doug Miller, he went back to the station raving about how great he was. Al and I chuckled about that, because, as chairman of the Gospel Announcer's Guild, he has been a long time supporter of gospel music.

We mainstreamed gospel music that day. It would still take several years before urban radio programmers and gospel music producers could reach common ground, but that was truly the beginning.

The Light Dims

By September of '85, not three months after the luncheon, a number of events occurred that would eventually lead to the downfall of Light Records. Ironically, the success of the Winans and the momentum generated at the BRE would eventually begin to work against the company.

Gene Whitman and Jay Franklin seemed to live in their own little world. The Burbank office they set up for themselves was two hours away in traffic from Light's main office and Roger Carlyle's ranch in Newberry Park.

Gene and Jay began to believe their own headlines. They began to believe their own slogan, "Light Records...The Artists' Company." In their infinite wisdom, Gene and Jay believed that their strategy of developing new artists was the route to go to increase market share. This was in direct contrast to Word's strategy of only putting out established artists. This emphasis on developing talent gave Gene more of an opportunity to flex his muscles as an A&R man, and Jay saw himself as an artist development person.

The truth is that Milton had become Jay Franklin's teacher and provided a natural buffer between me and Jay. Before Light, Jay Franklin was a missionary somewhere—he probably didn't even know there was a hole in a record. Now he wanted greater responsibility and authority, and they were looking to me to train him. *No way!* Since then, I've seen this scenario play itself out over and over again.

Also that month, Sheila had a baby and was preparing to move her company back East, and Milton left California to go back to New York to marry Pat Prescott, who was then the WBLS "morning drive" personality. That was the end of my buffer. I knew I was headed on a collision course with Jay Franklin and Light, because there was no way I was going to move back to Los Angeles to train this blockhead.

Gene and Jay were tripping, Sheila and Milton were out of the picture, I was at odds with the company—the stage was set for the backstabbers and the armchair advisors. Jack Murphy, a White salesman from Word, became the head of sales. John Marrs, who was Jacks's boy, took over the national promotion chores.

It was no secret that I was at odds with Light over the Jay Franklin situation. They actually wanted me to relocate back to California to train this guy so that he could become my boss. I had never heard anything so ridiculous. Things moved fast. I had a choice to relocate back to Los Angeles or work for Light as an independent. My role changed as I decided on the latter option—to stay on the East Coast and remain independent.

John Marrs saw what was going on, and along with Jack Murphy, conspired to push me out. Marrs successfully convinced Jay Franklin that they didn't need me as long as they had him.

As an extension of "the Artists' Company" strategy, Jack Murphy and John Marrs convinced Light to take on distribution of a lot of little labels including Command, Tyscot and I AM. Little did they realize that "I AM" was in fact Marrs' label. The net result was Jack Murphy was getting paid on both ends—from the labels and from Light.

Light Records' marketing resources were severely diluted. The manufacturing cost of their product skyrocketed. Inflated production costs became the last vestige of thievery, leaving the label penniless and broke. Within a year the label went from #1 to bankruptcy for the second and final time.

One thing is for sure, Light didn't go out on my watch. There was one testament to my leadership that nobody could deny. In January of 1986 the ballots for the '86 Grammy Awards came out (for 1985 releases). Under the heading "Best Soul Gospel Performance by a Duo, Group, Choir or Chorus," Light Records had *all five* nominations.

Epilogue: Just Business

That fall, when I was in Los Angeles for one of my last meetings with Light Records, I called up my old friend Cortez Thompson for a meeting at Warner Brothers Records in his Burbank office. The former WOL program director (The Golden Terror) was now the Senior Vice President of Promotion for Black Music at the label. It was good seeing Cortez again.

After exchanging pleasantries, I got down to business. I was on a mission. I was there to pitch Cortez on the Winans. I gave

Cortez a copy of the Winans *Tomorrow* album. I told him we pre-sold 50,000 units.

His response was, "We have some *secular* artists that don't sell *50,000!*"

At that point he called in Warner's Black marketing chief Oscar Fields, who brought in a bottle a vintage California Chardonay. We talked about the gospel market, Warner Brothers, and the Winans. By the time I left, three seeds had been planted. First, signing the Winans would be a bold and positive move for Warner Brothers. Second, contemporary gospel music, specifically the Winans, was ready to explode. Third, and perhaps most important, Vernice would work with the Winans from that day on.

Within six months the Winans were released on Quincy Jones' Warner Brothers-distributed label, Qwest. The project got the full backing of the Warner Brothers and WEA (Warner Brothers, Elektra and Atlantic Records Distribution) marketing machine, and the rest is history.

And yes, I was on the project.

In January 1987, one year after I left Light Records, I was sitting in a suite at the Parker Meridian Hotel in New York. The suite was being paid for by Aaron Glenn, mega concert promoter Quentin Perry, and Broadway aficionado Jeff Sharp. I was there working with my production partner, Jackie Burston, (Smokey Robinson's neice) on their Broadway production of *Don't Get God Started* starring Bebe Winans, Vanessa Bell-Armstrong and Chip Fields, with music by Marvin Winans. I was also working on the historic Winans Live at Carnegie Hall concert, which the trio was simultaneously promoting.

Quentin was an amazing businessman, and he always knew

how to turn other people's missed opportunities and misfortunes to his own advantage. It was that character trait that led me to the biggest account I ever had.

One of the standard advertisers in *Playbill,* the Broadway publication for legit theaters, was Revlon. Revlon had been having some problems because of a remark made by one of its senior executives regarding other Black hair care companies. It was enough to spark a boycott by Black beauty salons—with a little fanning of the flame from Jesse Jackson. It was also enough for Quentin Perry to push me to pitch Revlon as a potential sponsor. They wanted to take *Don't Get God Started* national.

I contacted James Alexander, Revlon's senior vice president of special markets. Most major consumer goods companies have "special markets" divisions that cater to the needs of the Black consumer market. I piqued his interest by telling him there was a beauty salon scene in the play, and we wanted to utilize Revlon products as props. I also invited the senior vice president of marketing and the group president to attend the show.

Once we knew we had their interest, the production team, Chip Fields, Aaron, Quentin and myself, put our heads together to decide the best way to maximize Revlon's potential involvement. From that point on, everything was staged. Chip instructed the propmaster to conspicuously position the Revlon products. The executives' seats were strategically selected to position them on the same side of the stage as the salon scene. We even made sure that the seats directly in front of them were not sold so their view would not be obstructed. I made sure that a photographer was primed and ready for the Revlon executives.

It worked perfectly. About a week later, James Alexander

came to the Longacre Theatre with Revlon's group president and a senior VP of marketing. Mr. Alexander was the only one who knew about the Revlon props. They loved the show and got a real charge out of seeing their product. Backstage we set up the perfect photo opportunity with the cast including Chip Fields and Bebe Winans. As an unexpected extra added touch, Bebe provided the icing on the cake by serenading them all the way to their limousine. I got the picture in the papers and Revlon provided advertising support for the show. That was the beginning of my long and prosperous relationship with Revlon.

After the show that night, I was looking out over Central Park from my hotel suite feeling as if I was walking on air. *I had really pulled it off.* I was thinking back to that meeting in Cortez' office. I remember thinking to myself, *I wasn't disloyal to Light because Light had been disloyal to me. It was business—just business.*

Chapter 3

The Dwarf vs. the Giant

This is the story of The Dwarf vs. the Giant. It is the story of how a gorilla pitted the fortunes of a small African American-owned marketing company against those of a multinational giant.

In September of 1993, AT&T, in an internal publication called Focus, printed an illustration depicting international telephone communications. The drawing featured caricatures of different peoples from around the world using the telephone. In Great Britain, there were men wearing kilts. Hawaiians wore grass skirts, in the Alps, people wore Bavarian garb, and so on. While other continents depicted humans using the phone, the African continent pictured an ape with a phone in its hand.

On that same day, Vernice Watson, the owner of Prestige & Associates, an African American marketing firm, was busy working hard promoting the soundtrack from the movie *The Bodyguard* to gospel radio stations. Little did she realize that that paper gorilla would eventually embroil her in a protracted legal battle with AT&T that would push her to the brink of financial ruin.

This is the story of *Prestige & Associates vs. American Telephone and Telegraph.*

Buzz at the Caucus

I was attending Congressman Kweisi Mfume's reception at the annual Congressional Black Caucus Legislative Conference. The reception was in the elegant Grand Ballroom of the Capitol Hill Hyatt. In my years in the record business, I have become an expert at how to get in and out of receptions in thirty minutes. Unless I'm working, my *m.o.* is always the same. First, I always look stunning. I had on a black Jones New York suit from Saks Fifth Avenue with sequins around the collar and the pockets. It was a one button suit with a delicate sequined trim around the camisole—the kind of suit that makes you hold your stomach in so tight you can barely breathe. You might not be able to breathe, but it sure hangs just right over your hips.

I wore a black pill box hat with one sequined button on the side. The hat was made especially for me by Kit's Millinery of Pikesville. Kit designs the hats for all the rich ladies from the East Coast who attend the Preakness. (The Preakness is the second jewel in horse racing's Triple Crown held in Baltimore at the Pimlico Race Track.) You can even see Kit on TV news around

Preakness time doing interviews about her hat designs.

The Chairman's Reception at the Black Caucus is the kind of evening when you bring out all your diamonds. I had on my diamond necklace and earrings that Marcus had given me last Christmas. Black M'Lady shoes with rhinestones in the heels finished off my ensemble.

When you're making an entrance you have to have your plastic smile, look graceful and be sharp. Hey, that's the role you have to play when you go to the Caucus—look gorgeous, and make sure every word out of your mouth is politically correct.

That night I was with my friend Marcus Taylor, an executive at a Madison Avenue advertising agency. I've always been in love with Marcus. He is about six-foot-two, really built, with a teasing tan. He must have a little bit of Antiguan in him, because even when he loses his tan, he looks like he still might have one. He's got that, you know how we used to say when we were young, "good hair"—with a touch of gray on the temples, which he actually hates, but I love. It makes him look distinguished—that Ron Dellums look.

Speaking of Ron Dellums—he's the second person I saw that night.

Marcus is one of those smooth New York guys who really should have been from L.A. He's a smart dresser. When you wear a suit to a black tie affair, you know that suit has to be sharp. He wore a black double breasted Italian wool suit with a fine pin stripe by Franco Tossi. His white shirt was a perfect fit, 100 percent cotton broadcloth with a long point collar and French cuffs. His 100 percent Italian silk tie—top quality. I know all about ties. Heaven knows, I've bought enough of them over the years. This kind of tie allowed the dimple to fold effortlessly because of the quality of the silk.

He always wears the right shoes. That night he wore those black Bally lace ups. You can tell a lot about a man by looking at his nails and his shoes. Marcus' were always impeccable. He topped it all off with his 14 carat gold diamond studded cuff links.

Marcus was from the right family, went to the right schools, had the right contacts. When he met me he got the right woman.

In the Grand Hyatt, a long escalator brings you directly to the ballroom entrance. This gives you a long time to make your grand entrance. You know that everybody down there is looking back up to see who's coming. Have that plastic smile ready, watch what you do with your hands, and don't fidget or touch your face.

As we entered the escalator for the ride down into the ballroom the first person I spotted was Vernon Simms, Kweisi's campaign manager and right hand man. He stood out because he's attractive, tall, about six-five, light complexion, always dresses sharp and has a beautiful smile.

As we walked up to the check-in table to greet Vernon, Marcus whispered in my ear, "Whenever you walk into a room, the place lights up." That's all I needed to hear. I turned to him and said, "I promise you we'll be out of here in half an hour." I get a glass of wine, I make the rounds, shake hands, pose for pictures and I'm gone. I was there just long enough for someone to say, "Vernice was here."

I don't remember that much about the reception, but I'll never forget that night because there was this buzz going around the reception. Everybody was talking about it. I couldn't quite grasp the whole story, but I knew it had something to do with AT&T and some gorilla. Whatever happened, AT&T had messed up.

The next morning, I was in the hotel in my silk pajamas, waiting for my usual room service breakfast of a toasted bagel, fresh fruit, a glass of grapefruit juice and a cup of hot hotel coffee. Marcus was sound asleep. He always likes to sleep late, especially when it's raining. It was raining up a storm that morning.

I'll never forget. I sat there with coffee in one hand and the *Washington Post* in the other. There it was just as bold as day. *AT&T Apologizes for 'Racist' Illustration.*

I had heard about it the night before, and now here it was, confirmed in print. I was so absorbed by the article that I never let go of my coffee, and it gradually spilled into my plate ruining my bagel.

That was the first time I cursed AT&T.

After I read the article, I said to myself, *They've got a nasty little public relations problem. This may be an opportunity for me.*

After all, I specialize in cleaning up other people's public relations problems, but this one was more like a disaster.

Revlon's sales got a significant boost when I helped them with Jesse Jackson's boycott. Maybe, just maybe, I could clean up AT&T's mess. They had a real bad image problem and that's what I do best, help people clean up their image problems.

The following week, September 27, 1993, I sent the letter.

It's customary to send pitch letters to corporations, ad agencies, public relations firms, record companies and the like. Most of the time no response is expected. After years of rejection letters, I had gotten into the habit of sending pitch letters to the top dogs at these corporations. By directing my correspondence to the CEO or president, I'd usually get some kind of response. I addressed the letter to Robert Allen, Chairman and CEO of AT&T.

About a week later, I got a call from Elaine Logan at AT&T in New York asking me to come in for a meeting. I figured they must be calling everybody back who had sent them a letter. I was caught totally by surprise. I had to stall them until I could get a hold of Milton. We needed time to write a proposal and do our research.

Milton Allen is one of the smartest people I know and one of my very best friends. He'd been doing a lot of my proposal writing and brochures. I am the creative one, the idea partner, and Milton is the one who puts it all on paper. He's a good bulls— artist. When it comes to doing business presentations and meetings, he's the best.

Milton is from one of the first families of Baltimore—very bourgeois. His father was one of the first Black elected officials in Baltimore as State Attorney and then a Judge of the Supreme Bench. Milton himself is one of those Howard University snobs. But he's a real nice guy, funny, pleasant to be around. In appearance, he looks like a shorter version of Herbie Hancock.

Milton was a product manager at Arista Records during the Aretha Franklin, Phyllis Hyman, Dionne Warwick, Kenny G, Kashif and Whitney Houston days. He's been independent since 1983 and now runs his own company, Prescott-Allen Enterprises, with his former wife. He's been involved in public relations, video production, talent negotiations, satellite stuff, you name it. The only problem with Milton is getting him to stay focused on one thing long enough to get the job done. When I get determined to do something, I just do it.

I started my research without him.

I remember going to the library to research the company. I commandeered a corner and just took over for a few days. I checked the Black newspapers to see what AT&T had been doing, what was being written about them, what they could do. Basically, I wanted to figure out what I could bring to the table. Over the next week I managed to get the basic proposal done, but I still needed Milton to put the finishing touches on it and refine our pitch.

A week later I was in New York. It was the day of the presentation, and it was still difficult getting Milton to cooperate with me. He was preoccupied with producing his music videos and whatever else he was doing. He was really sending me through some trauma. He didn't finish his part of the proposal until the morning of the presentation. Then he didn't show up with his four critical pages until fifteen minutes before we were supposed to arrive at AT&T.

Fifteen minutes! He was driving me crazy. I was really stressed out. I could have killed him right on the spot, but I needed him for the presentation. I managed to maintain my composure, and we were on our way to the new AT&T building on Fifth Avenue. Fortunately, by the time we got to AT&T *they* were running late. I actually had time to sit down, compose myself and read what we were about to present.

The Presentation

The meeting was with Dick Martin, AT&T's vice president of public relations, and Esther Novak, who was obviously way down on one of the lower rungs of AT&T's corporate ladder.

The first person we encountered was a Black receptionist. In her young and perky way, she told us, "Mr. Martin is running late coming from the Basking Ridge, New Jersey headquarters."

A little later, Esther Novak showed up, apologized again for being late and escorted us down the hall to a conference room. We passed several offices on the way, and there wasn't another Black face in sight. (Whenever possible we try to get in a little early to see the conference room before the presentation. It's good to get a feel for the corporate environment.)

Esther led us into the conference room, then excused herself. The first thing we did was figure out where to sit. Where you sit relative to the other people in the room and each other is really important. You have to be comfortable. Milton and I usually try to sit we where can observe everything and play off each other. He usually ends up sitting on my right.

When Dick Martin walked in, he apologized and announced that he was expecting an overseas phone call. He was tall and lanky, not a lot of color to his skin. It was probably a call from his wife, stockbroker or somebody. They always run that international call game. We had just gotten started when the receptionist popped in and announced the call, so when he left the room, Milton seized the opportunity to interrogate Esther.

I don't think Esther was prepared for a Milton Allen interrogation. It was as if she was hypnotized. She answered everything he asked her. The first question was. "So Esther, how long have you been with AT&T."

By the time Milton finished, we not only knew Esther's entire history with the company, but a few other choice items as well. One thing we learned is that AT&T didn't have a clue how to handle the situation. She also let us know that the situation was worse than we had been led to believe. I'm sure she wasn't supposed to tell us, but apparently they were getting a lot of service cancellations because of this whole mess.

It didn't surprise me that she gave up all that information. She looked as though she was really stressed out. She reminded me of a cartoon character that just got an electric shock.

When we do presentations we take our cues from the people we are talking to. We can be relaxed and friendly or formal and cold. We chose the formal route. Milton took the lead. He does the play-by-play, I do the color. As we were going through the presentation, I saw that we were losing Martin. I was trying to figure out how to handle this when the receptionist popped her head in again to say the "such and such agency is waiting."

Martin turned to her and barked, "Can't you see we're in the middle of a meeting? They will have to wait."

It bothered me to be interrupted like that, because you lose your focus. If we had been a White firm, would she have interrupted? I guess those people in the lobby must having been worrying her to death.

The break in his concentration gave me an opportunity. I put the paper down and started to ad-lib. I snapped him out of it by saying, "Dick, picture this." I held up my hands like a movie director and I began to graphically describe my concept for the commercials we were proposing. I actually started singing.

Milton was totally amazed. I remember him turning all the way around in his chair as if to say, *Have you lost your mind?!* First I was a choir, then I was the Winans, then Anita Baker, then Whitney Houston. I explained to him that what they should do is to get someone who is truly unique to epitomize their concept of "true voice." That would get them the backing of Black radio. I was trying to get him to conceptualize their existing commercial campaigns with a Black flavor.

After listening intently, Martin announced, "We have no budget."

We were used to that response, and we knew exactly how to handle it. As if on cue, Milton dramatically set the papers aside, looked Martin right in the eye and said, "Here's our pitch." He broke it down to its simplest denominator and made it crystal-clear what we were talking about.

"Tailor your advertising messages to relate to the Black consumer market by using recognized celebrities like Whitney Houston, and combine this with relevant community-based public service programs." We suggested that they could reallocate dollars from existing campaigns to fund this meager effort. After all, if they didn't have any money, why were we there?

When it was all said and done, Dick Martin said that the ideas we'd presented sounded "...very intriguing." He had to snap Esther out of her trance by asking her if she had any questions, to which she replied with a glazed look, "Do you have any references?"

We knew we had them where we wanted them. We knew we had AT&T!

I called everyone from whom they wanted a reference. It was a Who's Who list of Black executives—Tony Anderson, Senior Vice President and General Manager SONY Music; Eddie Pugh, Vice President SONY Music; James Alexander, Senior Vice President Revlon; Glynice Coleman, Senior Vice President EMI Records; Doug Daniel, Senior Vice President Arista Records; and of course, my best friend, Jean Alston from Great Bay Distributors in Baltimore.

I called everybody, told them about the presentation and told them, "Make me look good." Then I called Kweisi's Mfume's office to ask him to send a recommendation letter. He sent an awesome letter to AT&T, saying I could "...play a pivotal role in improving their image."

COMMITTEES:
Banking, Finance & Urban Affairs
Small Business
Joint Economic Committee
Select Committee on Narcotics

SUB-COMMITTEES:
Housing & Community Development
Financial Institutions Supervision
SBA and the General Economy

MEMBER:
Congressional Black Caucus
Caucus on Women's Issues
Congressional Arts Caucus
Federal Government
Service Task Force
Task Force on Homelessness

Congress of the United States
House of Representatives
Washington, D.C. 20515

KWEISI MFUME
7TH DISTRICT, MARYLAND

WASHINGTON OFFICE:
217 Cannon Building
Washington, D.C. 20515
202/225-4741

DISTRICT OFFICES:
3000 Druid Park Drive
Baltimore, MD 21215
410/367-1900

1825 Woodlawn Drive
Suite 106
Baltimore, MD 21207
410/298-5997

2203 N. Charles Street
Baltimore, MD 21218
410/235-2700

4 November 1993

Robert Allen, Chairman and CEO
American Telephone and Telegraph Company
295 North Maple Avenue
Basking Ridge, NJ 07920

Dear Mr. Allen,

I am writing you on behalf of Vernice Watson, an owner of Prestige and Associates. Ms. Watson recently met with employees of American Telephone and Telegraph Company (A.T.& T.) regarding a Proposal for services.

Ms. Watson's Proposal is an attempt to maintain your company's strong and positive image among African American consumers. To achieve this goal, Ms. Watson is uniquely suited to play a pivotal role in the gospel market's approach to this effort.

I respectfully request that you review this Proposal and hope that this project meets your approval.

Sincerely,

Kweisi Mfume
Member of Congress

KM/vs

A few days later I got a call from Patrice Glenn in AT&T's Creative Services Department. She said she was reviewing my proposal, and it was extremely good. I knew this was a good sign. She said she needed me to help prepare her for a meeting so she could get money to implement some of the recommendations. She told me that the company was very interested in the Stellar Awards, and that they wanted to advertise. She even asked me to call Central City Productions, the company that produces the Stellars, to ask them to hold up their deadline so they could advertise. The Stellar Awards are the gospel version of the Grammys. The show is produced by Don Jackson of Central City Productions in Chicago and is syndicated nationally by Tribune Entertainment.

I called Milton to tell him how excited I was about what was going on. His only comment was, "How do you know AT&T won't just use your stuff and leave you in the dust?"

Here I was on the verge of getting the biggest account of my life, and all he could say was, *How do you know they won't steal your stuff?*

I had to stop talking to Milton for a while. I just did not want to hear it. I was incredibly focused. The whole time, the thought never occurred to me *he could be right.* For the first time in my life, I had to turn Milton off.

In the meantime, I mentally and emotionally prepared myself for the AT&T account. Prestige had finally arrived! First, the record business, then Revlon, and now, AT&T. *How sweet it is!*

I assembled my team—Milton, Eilene Lifsey-Towns, Jean Alston, April Washington, and Dawn Brooks. Each had their own specialty. Eilene was the best at event management and public relations, Jean and April were experts in radio and music marketing, Dawn Brooks was a computer genius and Milton, well, he does everything.

One week later, Tony Anderson from SONY Music called to say he hadn't heard from AT&T. "What was going on?" he asked.

I said, "Everything is going great, and I'm working on the Stellars for them." Tony interrupted me and asked point blank, "Do you have a contract?"

He had busted me, and I couldn't say a word. That was my second alarm. Now two of my friends, Milton and Tony, were giving me warning signals. But I never really heard them. All I could see was the great, wonderful world of almighty AT&T.

Heather Davis and Don Jackson at the Stellars got excited about the AT&T thing. They faxed me tons of documents—market information, Neilsen numbers, program descriptions, you name it. My office was filling up with fax paper. And like a good little soldier, *I dutifully faxed it on to AT&T.* And to think that girl at AT&T actually told me that I was helping "prepare" her.

By now, I wasn't calling Milton any more, but he was calling me. Every time I told him what was going on, he would just argue more. But I just wasn't getting it. As far as I was concerned, Milton was being negative, and I didn't have time to deal with negative attitudes. So I just tuned him out.

I called Joyce Logan at *Gospel International Magazine* and asked her to kill the gorilla follow-up story she was working on. *She did.*

Three weeks went by, and the Stellar taping was about to happen. Heather Davis from Central City Productions was calling me daily. After all, for a new nationally syndicated show like the Stellars, AT&T was a *big* deal.

I became just a little bit uncomfortable with the AT&T situation. But I wrote it off as their being this lumbering corporate giant, and figured, *This must be the way they do business.* The worst part of it was I still had to hear Milton's mouth. I decided I was not going to call AT&T anymore. The taping came—and went.

The very next day after the taping, I got a call from Esther Novak. It was a strange and disconcerting phone call. First of all, she sounded as if she was on a car phone somewhere (the connection was lousy), and she was upset. She sounded like she was crying. I later found out that she had apparently just been told she was being fired.

Poor Esther. *C'est la vie.*

She told me AT&T was not going to do the Stellars and that my new contact person was going to be Charlene Brown. This did not come as a surprise to me even though, up until that moment, I still held out hope that AT&T would still come through. Even though the show had already been taped, AT&T still could have been inserted during the editing process. The worst part of it was I had to tell Heather that AT&T was not coming through.

I never really, *really* wanted to believe I was getting the runaround, but every time I began to get that feeling, a new player emerged. And every time a new player emerged, I had new hope.

Charlene Brown was the National Manager Public Relations, African American, Caribbean & African Markets. With a title that long, I knew I was in high-cotton now. I never met her, but I knew, or at least I thought, she was Black. Charlene was my *fifth* AT&T contact. By now, I was beginning to become suspicious. I actually began to believe that AT&T had Whites masquerading on the phone as Blacks.

I spent a lot of time on the phone with Charlene. She reiterated that my proposal was good, but they wanted to wait until after the holidays. "We're restructuring our department, recovering from Esther being fired," she said.

You know what the bottom line is? Everybody at AT&T was brain-dead. Nobody had a creative cell in their brain. They didn't have a clue about Black people. Charlene didn't even have a clue about her job. All they wanted to do was pump me for information—and stall me. And that's just what she did!

Oh, she had that AT&T charm. She would occasionally drop that veneer and be a sister just so I'd think she was on my side. Just another dance. But when you think about it, why would she be on *my* side? AT&T was paying her, not me.

At the beginning of December I received a letter from Charlene with the AT&T Foundation's Annual Report and a video tape set, *AT&T in the Black Community*. In the letter, she asked me to contact her after Christmas. Like clockwork, I contacted her right after Christmas. She told me to call her back in February. She would be interested in using our services at that time. This should have been a big clue. I should have realized that they were just "slow walking" me, stalling. But why?

It was a classic case of not being able to see the forest for the trees. The closer it got to the holidays, the wearier I grew of AT&T and Milton's mouth. I must admit I was starting to listen to him, though.

I had had enough of Miss Charlene Brown when one day I got a call from Vernon Sims of Kweisi Mfume's Capitol Hill office. Vernon called to tell me that some guy from AT&T, Earl Unikel, called to get my number. Vernon and I assumed that he called just to see if Kweisi really knew me.

Earl Unikel was the Director of Minority & Women Business. Now I knew I was where I was supposed to be. He and I hit it off very well on the phone. He was very encouraging. He told me how he was going to guide me through the AT&T maze. He said, "If you hang in there and not give up, you will eventually get in." For the moment that was good enough for me.

December and January came and went. I called Charlene Brown. She asked me to be patient, because she was waiting for a new department head. Then she would schedule a meeting. Right!

Another month went by. No meeting, no calls, no nothing. The only time I got a reaction from AT&T is when I got on the phone. All I wanted them to do is what they said they would do. That's it—period! I decided it was time for me to retake the initiative and start to press AT&T for some answers. I made several follow-up calls, and after several phone conversations with Earl Unikel, I scheduled a March 11th meeting. The meeting was later postponed to April 8th.

April 4th, I called Charlene Brown. She asked me to contact Linda Dukette or Herman Morales at Uniworld, AT&T's "Black" advertising agency of record. Uniworld turned out to be another dead end. More phone calls, more questions, more referrals—dead end. I finally decided to call my friend, Walker Williams, head of the Uniworld office in Washington, D.C.

I met Walker on a ten-day fact finding trip to South Africa.

The tour included other media people such as Paul Majors, owner of WTMP in Tampa; Debra Crable from the Ebony Jet Showcase TV show, and others. But that's another story for another chapter. Anyway, Walker said he would see what he could find out from Byron Lewis, the owner/CEO of Uniworld, and get back to me.

It looked as if my first best hope was Earl Unikel. He was saying all the right things. "Be patient. I'll walk you through it. They're still considering your proposals." We had some things in common. We talked about the music business, Black music, and his favorite artists. I knew he was going to be my *Black knight in shining armor* and get me through the AT&T maze.

On April 8th, 1994, I got a big surprise. My Black knight in shining armor turned out to be White, short, bald, and wearing a golf outfit. That meeting was a little odd because it was Friday—dress down day at AT&T. Here I was in my Black Cache suit with matching hat, shoes, and bag, sitting across from this bald-headed, golf-outfit-wearing man.

The meeting did seem to go well, though. Unikel talked about how to navigate through AT&T and how he would personally do his best to get answers from Dick Martin's office, because he thought I had "great ideas."

April went by, then May. Right before Memorial Day I got a message on my voice mail from Earl Unikel:

"Vernice. Hi. This is Earl Unikel. How're you doing? I am pursuing that matter on your proposal. I called Dick Martin's office, and I am also trying to talk to Charlene Brown just to follow up on some questions that I left with them a while back. So I think it is just a matter of us trying to connect up…get people to stop playing phone tag. I am waiting for a call back from them. Based on my last discussion with them, they were not ready to do anything. So I want you to know that this is not the first time I talked to them. But let me see what they say when I talk to them again. Then, hopefully, I will be able to call you back in a few days. Thanks a lot."

Black Friday

I will never forget the day, June 17, 1994—Black Friday. That was the day my girlfriend, April, called me to tell me AT&T was going to use Whitney Houston for their "True Voice" commercial and that it was scheduled to premiere on Entertainment Tonight *that night.*

As I watched the show, I literally got sick to my stomach. As soon as it was over, I didn't waste any time. I left urgent voice mail messages with everyone—Earl Unikel, Charlene Brown, Dick Martin, the whole lousy bunch. I now realized that the whole time, they were just playing with me. They were just stalling me and keeping me preoccupied until they could finish the commercial.

The next working day, June 20th, Earl Unikel was the first to call back. He had developed a case of amnesia. He said he thought the artist I had suggested was Howard Hewett, not Whitney Houston. So much for Earl Unikel.

I called Dick Martin and left another urgent message for him to call me regarding Whitney Houston and "True Voice." I was on my way to Towson Town Center to go shopping when I checked my voice mail to find he had returned my call. I called him from the car to ask what was going on?

"Why were they using my concept without asking me, and more importantly, *not paying me?*" I pleaded.

I told him I thought that Uniworld had stolen my idea. Dick Martin said in defense of their agency, "Uniworld didn't steal your idea. We went directly to Whitney Houston in December." I reminded him that I presented that very idea to him in October.

I'll never ever forget his response.

"Well, one thing about a good idea, more than one person may have it."

My response, "We will see."

That was the last time I spoke to Dick Martin.

We Will See

The first call I made after that was to Whitney Houston's executive administrator, Robin Crawford. Robin told me unequivocally that AT&T did not contact Whitney until April. She was certain, because she had the dated correspondence pinned up on her bulletin board.

The second call I made was to Walker Williams who had just spoken to Byron Lewis, President of Uniworld in New York. Walker quoted Lewis as saying, "The first time I saw it was in the *New York Times.* They gave it to the White boys."

My third call was to my good friend Doug Daniel, Senior Vice President of Promotion at Arista, Whitney's Record Company. He said the first he had heard of it was in May.

I knew that I had a fight on my hands—a big fight. I knew I would have to go to "the lawyers."

Chapter 4

The Lawyers

AFTER THREE LAW FIRMS AND OVER $100,000,
I'M BACK WHERE I STARTED.

After *Entertainment Tonight* aired, my phone started ringing off the hook. They all knew that it was my idea and were calling to congratulate me. Even my hairdresser, Queenie, called to congratulate me. Vernon Simms, Congressman Kweisi Mfume's campaign manager, called. Doug Daniel from Whitney's record company, Arista, and all my friends from the record business called. *Can anyone ever imagine what I felt?* I was getting nowhere fast trying to call AT&T and make sense out of all this. Earl Unikel was trying to convince me to be patient and to "work within the system."

We wrote to AT&T several times, and finally they sent me a contract to sign after the fact. After careful inspection, I found it wasn't a contract at all. *It was a generic release form that abdicated all rights to my creative ideas to AT&T.* No way! After I refused to sign such an onerous document, they conceded they would talk to me, provided that two concessions were met: (1) that I would not discuss it with anyone, and (2) that I come to the table with an attorney.

BEWARE OF THE ARMCHAIR ADVISORS

I was getting unsolicited advice from everybody. One particular piece of bad advice came from my girlfriend Theresa Cain's *neighbor* who works with the EEOC. Theresa, who is always very resourceful, insisted I discuss the situation with him. This guy suggested that I send AT&T an invoice for services rendered. After all, if they wanted me to sign a contract after the fact, they would certainly entertain an invoice. So I sent them an invoice for $100,000.

Then, *where I probably made my biggest mistake,* I got excited. Everyone was pumping me up. The EEOC guy suggested I send them an invoice that was closer to the dollar value of the Whitney Houston advertising campaign.

On July 18, 1994, I sent a corrected invoice for $3.5 million.

Well, needless to say, they could not handle it. If I knew then what I know now, I would have taken the $100,000 and called it a day. I'd have my second house by now.

Normally, I would not have taken someone's advice so blindly. I never even checked this guy out. I just followed his advice because he was Theresa's friend, and he worked at the EEOC. For all I know, he could have been a janitor. But circumstances were far from normal. I was becoming obsessed with AT&T.

July 18, 1994

Mr. Dick Martin
Vice President Public Relations
American Telephone and Telegraph Company
205 North Maple Avenue
Basking Ridge, New Jersey 07290

Dear Mr. Martin:

    We had hoped to develop a long-term relationship with your company. Because of this expectancy, we were very candid in our discussions with you and your staff during meetings last year and more recently in 1994. As I expressed to you in recent phone conversations, we were very disappointed to see our proposals enacted without our company being involved or compensated.
    As you know, our ideas are our primary asset, and when we speak freely to you and anyone else and submit detailed proposals, we expect fairness and ethical treatment in return.
    We are submitting the attached invoice for payment as we feel it is a reasonable fee for the programs developed for your company.

                              Sincerely yours,
                              Vernice Watson

cc: Mr. Robert Allen, Chairman and CEO
      Mr. Kenneth Thompson, Piper & Marbury
      The Honorable Kweisi Mfume, Member of Congress
      Mr. Earl Unikel, Director of Minority & Women
          Businesses

    All my friends started calling me, referring me to different law firms. I contacted at least 10 different firms. None of them wanted to take the case. None of them were willing to use their resources to go to battle with AT&T. I called lawyers, from Baltimore attorney Kenneth Thompson to Clinton confidant and perennial Washington insider Vernon Jordan. Mr. Jordon did not return my call. In fact, whenever you call a law firm and mention you want them to represent you against AT&T, you can count on not getting a call back.

Then my friend, Wayne Cooper, suggested I call E. Scott Johnson from Ober, Kaler, Grimes & Shriver. Out of all the people I spoke to, E. Scott Johnson was the kindest and the most helpful. He said my case had settlement value and that I could sue AT&T under intellectual property law.

Frances Jones

I began my own research on intellectual property law. But still I could not find a law firm that would go up against AT&T.

Finally, my friend and client Raina Bundy, then a vice president from Columbia Records in New York, called Frances Jones and asked her, as a personal favor, to take my case. Raina helped me because she saw that it was ruining my career, that I was becoming obsessed, and that it was taking away from what I did best—marketing and promoting music. It also affected her personally because, at the time, Sony Music was the parent company of Columbia records, one of my biggest clients. Raina even rushed through one of my invoices so I could pay the retainer for Frances' legal services.

August 15, 1994

Ms. Vernice Watson, President
Prestige & Associates
1312 Idylwood Road
Pikesville, MD 21208

Dear Ms. Watson:

    I was surprised to receive your July 18, 1994 letter and accompanying invoice. We are unaware of any consulting work or programs you have developed for AT&T or any ideas which originated with you or your company that were used by AT&T. Consequently, we cannot pay your invoice.

    If you believe you have provided services to AT&T, I should appreciate it if you would supply a detailed listing of services and the AT&T business units that received such services. We will then consider your claim and respond promptly.

                                Sincerely yours,
                                Richard J. Martin

Frances did all the ground work. She researched the case thoroughly and interviewed everyone from Vernon Sims at Kweisi's office to Rev. Buster Soaries of Proclaim Records (who had received a large grant from AT&T). Most of his central New Jersey congregation were AT&T employees. Frances was so sure it was a good case. She told me it was a "...great case worth a lot of money."

When I asked Frances how much money, she said, "Seven figures."

August 24, 1994

Mr. Dick Martin
Vice President Public Relations
American Telephone and Telegraph Company
295 North Maple Avenue
Basking Ridge, NJ 07920

Dear Mr. Martin:

    Your response to our letter is not acceptable. We are again requesting payment of our July 18 invoice.
    I remind you that during the course of our meetings with you and your staff in October 1993, we pitched certain ideas. It is clear that you implemented, utilized and exploited proposals, presentations, concept research and intellectual property presented to you by Prestige & Associates.
    Mr. Martin, it is always preferable to settle a dispute of this nature without litigation. However, within seven days I will forward this invoice and the entire AT&T file to my attorneys for immediate action.
    We expect to hear from you soon.

                              Sincerely yours,
                              Vernice Watson

Frances said AT&T wouldn't want the publicity, and they would most likely settle out of court, probably before Christmas.

I was ecstatic. I went shopping for the first time in months. I went to Cache and bought a $400 suit. I even called Frances before I bought it. She encouraged me to get it. "You can go shopping," were her exact words. And go shopping I did.

I even went to look at houses, because I knew this AT&T money was coming in. I planned on relocating to Atlanta and building an Ashley home in the fashionable Stone Mountain area. Even my old boss from Word, Jonas Boston, then general manager at Intersound Records in Atlanta, and Vanessa Vaughn from Inspirations Across America, the nationally syndicated gospel radio show out of Atlanta, were both looking for homes for me. I was so obsessed by this whole thing, I had planned my 4,000 square foot (not including the basement) dream home down to the last square inch.

When you walk into my AT&T home, you enter into a two-story foyer with a formal living room on the right, at least 14 by 17 feet. My dining room, on the left side of the foyer, isn't really that big—maybe 12 by 15 because I only do formal entertaining during the Christmas holidays. Marcus says I should use the dining room as a boardroom. I have a library on the first floor with an adjacent sun room. I do all my entertaining in my family room which is big and near the kitchen so that when my brothers Alvin and Stanley come over to watch the playoff games and the fights, they don't drag food all over my thick plush carpets.

Upstairs, my master bedroom suite is at least 19 by 15 feet with a 10 by 9 sitting room and a walk-in dressing room that's at least 15 by 15. That room has enough custom-built shelving to hold 100 hat boxes and at least 100 pairs of shoes. My garden master bathroom has skylights, a huge sunken tub and double sinks with mirrors. My office is in the basement with an exercise room, a media room and a walkout where you can walk up to a two level deck off the kitchen. And, of course, my AT&T home is located on a wooded lot large enough for the three-car side load garage.

In the garage is a champagne colored Jaguar XJ-12 sedan and a black Jeep Grand Cherokee with a gold package (that's how I get around in the wintertime).

Oh God, what a dream! Frances was so sure. How could she have been so wrong?

September 23, 1994

Mr. Dick Martin
Vice President Public Relations
American Telephone and Telegraph Company
295 North Maple Avenue
Baskin Ridge, New Jersey 07920

Dear Mr. Martin:

We have had no response from you since our letter of August 22nd. Although you state that you are "unaware" of any ideas which originated with me, at least three ideas that were included in our proposal presentation have been implemented. This cannot be mere coincidence.

1. We referred your company to the Black Radio Exclusive Convention and you participated for the first time this year.

2. We suggested using an African-American recording artist to represent "Your True Voice" (Whitney Houston was specifically suggested as an artist that we worked with and was suggested because she has a distinctive voice and cross-over appeal in both secular and gospel markets).

3. We suggested that you be represented at the Gospel Music Workshop of America "1994 - The Year of Gospel Music." You participated this year.

Mr. Martin, it would be clear to any reasonable person that your company utilized elements of our proposal submitted to you last year and that reasonable compensation is due us. We are not familiar enough with your internal organization to identify the specific business units that implemented the above activity.

We realize that AT&T is a corporate giant and we are only a very small business without the financial resources available to you. However, we believe that ultimately, we can secure payment through litigation if necessary.

We ask only that you be fair with us in the resolution of this matter.

Sincerely,
Vernice Watson

cc: Mr. Robert Allen, Chairman and CEO
Mr. Kenneth Thompson, Piper & Marbury
The Honorable Kweisi Mfume, Member of Congress
Mr. Earl Unikel, Director of Minority & Women Businesses
Mr. Nicholas Coch, Esq., Rogers & Wells

During my research, I kept coming across the name Nicholas Coch, as a prominent authority on intellectual property law. I called his office and left a message—of course, no response. So to intimidate AT&T, I copied Coch on the letter, and I did fax him a copy.

After several discussions with AT&T, Frances Jones realized that she was not getting anywhere and that they were just stalling.

October 5, 1994

Ms. Vernice Watson, President
Prestige & Associates
1312 Idylwood Road
Pikesville, Md. 21208

Dear Ms. Watson:

Thank you for your letter of September 23, 1994.
We do not believe that the three ideas listed in your letter are sufficiently concrete or original to give rise to any legal claim. Furthermore, your letter still does not provide the detailed listing of services we previously requested (including

the dates you claim to have provided such services to AT&T).

However, AT&T is committed to the amicable resolution of disputes. In this spirit we would be willing to meet with you and your attorney, but only under the following conditions.

First, you must be represented by counsel (I note that you sent copies of your letters to Kenneth Thompson, Esq., of Piper and Marbury, and Nicholas Koch, Esq., of Rogers and Wells). Second, you must agree that the meeting and what is discussed at the meeting will be confidential.

If you wish to proceed under these conditions, please have your attorney call either Frank Politano, Esq. at [phone number] or Bernard Zucker, Esq. at [phone number], both of the AT&T Law Department, to set up a meeting.

          Sincerely,
          Richard J. Martin

Almost one year had gone by since Milton and I first sat down with Dick Martin and Esther Novak. One year and still no settlement. When we made that presentation I felt like I was at the top of my game. To do something that good and to see it on TV and hear it on radio all the time was driving me crazy. I couldn't stand the thought of being denied my proper credit. Every time I heard that True Voice commercial, I became physically ill. I would actually throw up. I love Whitney Houston. But I could not stand hearing that commercial.

Some of my friends stopped talking to me, because that's all I talked about. I felt sorry for Jean Alston more than anybody else. Because she was my best friend, we would talk sometimes five times a day. All I wanted to do was verbalize my plight with AT&T. It took a lot out of me and it took a lot out of my business. I got so caught up in AT&T, I lost some of my momentum. I didn't know it then, but I was slowly sinking into a deep depression as my preoccupation with AT&T took over my psyche.

All my hopes were now pinned on Frances. She tried everything. She even threatened them with a press conference and to bring in a list of 20 "who's who in the music industry" for witnesses. She threatened them with depositions. She threatened them with a public scandal. But they did not bite. She had had enough when she dropped the following communique:

Via Certified Mail
October 28, 1994

Mr. Dick Martin
Vice-President Public Relations
American Telephone and Telegraph Company
295 North Maple Avenue, Suite 2329
Basking Ridge, New Jersey 07920

Re: Prestige & Associates *v.* AT&T/claims re: Whitney Houston campaign, etc.

Dear Mr. Martin:

Please be advised that this firm has been retained to represent Prestige & Associates in the above-referenced matter, and all future correspondence should be addressed to the Austin, Texas address indicated above.

Based upon our extensive review of the overwhelming amount of physical, testimonial and documentary evidence in existence, (including, without limitation, various tape recordings and ample supporting documentation in great detail of all meetings, conversations, correspondence and corroborating witnesses), we are prepared to clearly and unequivocally demonstrate American Telephone and Telegraph Company's ("AT&T"s) use of my clients ideas and services, including, without limitation, those outlined in the written proposal submitted to AT&T in the meeting with you on October 14,

1993 and those verbally communicated to you and other AT&T representatives during such meeting and thereafter.

In view of the enormous benefits which AT&T has and is enjoying as a direct result of my client's good faith efforts on its behalf, it is absolutely ludicrous, astounding and appalling that you would consider for a moment not properly compensating it.

Is this yet another demonstration of AT&T's "true colors"?

Although we have not yet done so, we are prepared to enlist a venerable WHO'S WHO list of over twenty (20) extremely high profile, highly respected recording, radio and print media executives and politicians, all of whom could readily testify as to and corroborate my client's credible professional reputation throughout the community and the chain of events concerning AT&T's use of my clients and efforts including, without limitation, the use of Whitney Houston as its new "true voice."

We feel that the upcoming holiday season would provide my client with an ideal opportunity to receive broad-based coverage and support in publicizing the outrageous insult which AT&T has dealt it and in once again allowing the public to view AT&T's "true colors" with respect to individuals and businesses of color.

As I am sure you are aware, the orchestration of such a full-blown press blitz would completely undermine the purpose and effectiveness of the Houston campaign, and would only serve to greatly increase my client's visibility, credibility and respectability throughout the community.

We are seeking the following: a) Three Million Five Hundred Thousand Dollars (U.S. $3,500,000.00) due and owing; b) accord Prestige & Associates appropriate credit; and c) a future five (5) year contract with AT&T.

It is understood that we are prepared to proceed in good faith with discussions towards this end. You should be aware that we are interested in resolving this disputed matter in an expeditious fashion.

However, please be advised that in order to protect my client's rights and interests, our failure to resolve this matter in a positive fashion may necessitate a federal filing, which, as you know, would also be subject to public disclosure.

We anticipate a timely response arranging a telephone conference meeting at your earliest convenience, but not later than Thursday, November 10, 1994 at 5:00 p.m. Pacific Standard Time. I may be reached most directly at 213/ 939.4205.

Of course, this letter is written without prejudice to any of my client's rights and/or remedies at law and/or equity, all of which rights and/or remedies are hereby expressly reserved without limitation or exception.

Sincerely,
Frances J. Jones

When she read the letter to me I got chills, it was worded so strongly. I imagined Frances dropping this letter on AT&T as analogous to the U.S. dropping the atomic bomb on Nagasaki.

But AT&T had their bomb squad out that day. They must have some contingency plan for dealing with threatening lawyers. Frances' atomic bomb turned out to be an atomic dud. There was no press conference, no broad-based coverage, no who's who, no federal filing and certainly no check or contract.

AT&T assigned two attorneys to Frances—Bernard Zucker and some other ball-buster whose name escapes me. They must have been AT&T's "crazy lawyer squad." After all, for one lawyer to go up against AT&T single handedly with a bunch of threats, they must be crazy. They did what I now know as the classic "AT&T stall." They had several telephone conferences with Frances. They made her think they were actually negotiating various points. Frances would call me up and give me progress reports and updates. I was living from phone call to phone call, waiting for any late breaking news from my attorney.

I was on the road promoting a Motown Records compilation called *Motown Comes Home*. On a promotional tour, you always sit with the artist when they are in the studio to make sure they say the right things, thank the right people and don't forget where they are. Since this was a compilation album, I was on the road with legendary Motown producer Frank Wilson. As soon as I got Frank seated in the studio, I would take off, find the nearest pay phone and call Frances to find out what was going on. I was just waiting to hear how much they were settling for.

I was at the point where I would go for just about anything that would make money—just hoping and praying AT&T would come through. A friend of mine introduced me to AMCALL, a multilevel phone card business. Although it was very uncharacteristic of me, I actually agreed to go to an AMCALL meeting in Charlotte, North Carolina. I always use travel time to go through my unopened mail, so on my way to the airport I was reading my mail, and there was the *Black Radio Exclusive* magazine. It was BRE publisher Sidney Miller's convention review issue. I was floored when I saw that AT&T was at the convention.

"They stole my idea again!" I screamed. I thought back to that ill-fated presentation, and I remembered vividly explaining to Dick Martin the value of participating in the BRE convention. I immediately got on the phone and left "urgent" messages for Sidney Miller.

Sidney called me from Aretha Franklin's suite at the Hyatt Regency in Atlanta. I told him the whole story. He said he would help me anyway he could. He said he wasn't completely satisfied with their participation anyway. "I wanted them to talk about the information superhighway, and all they wanted to do was sell long distance," Sidney said.

I was obsessed. I couldn't even focus properly on new business, or current business for that matter. Eddie Pugh called me about working with Deniece Williams at Black Entertainment Television (BET). This would have been an easy $500. All I had to do was take Deniece over to BET and make sure everything went smoothly—that's it. But I could not focus on anything but my situation with AT&T.

Normally, I'd figure out how to get more than one thing done at a time. I always work on more than one project, and often I am required to be at more than one place at the same time. It's simple. You find the right person for the job and you delegate. But I couldn't get it together. It seemed only one task, outside of worrying, was all I could handle now.

I called Frances three to four times a day. She told me a lot of this and that, but still nothing spoke to my central question—where is the check? It finally became apparent to me and Frances that handling AT&T was beyond her means. She was too radical. They wouldn't deal with her. She was still telling me it was a good case, but in order to fight AT&T she would have to bring in some of her associates—some *good ol' boys* from Texas, as she described them.

SULLIVAN, ALBERT & BRAUN

Frances brought in the good old boys. The lead lawyer from Sullivan, Albert & Braun was Lester Weiss. I was told by Les it was a great case. They felt they could win it.

They said they had already won a couple of cases against AT&T representing MCI. They told me they didn't take on cases they did not think they could win. Then they played the Jewish Lawyer card. "We can talk to these guys," I was told. They sent a letter to AT&T asking them to come back to the table with a "dispassionate attitude."

The arrival of the SA&B gave me new hope. At last, a bright spot! But now, I had to figure out how to at least pay *their* expenses. Of course, they fly first class, stay in five star hotels, all on my money. They were probably triple billing me and other clients for those same expenses. (Yes, I saw *The Firm,* too). After this experience, I don't put anything past lawyers.

AT&T sent them a letter asking me to come to New York for a settlement meeting.

The Settlement Meeting

New York, here I come. I went through the expense of flying to New York and getting a hotel room to attend the settlement meeting. I'm thinking, *This thing is finally going to end.* Again, I became excited. I was happy in the true sense of the word. My only question was, *I wonder how much the check will be?*

It was a great day for a settlement. The sun was shining, I looked good, I was confident. Everything was going to be perfect. All my friends were encouraging me.

Even my friend Pat Prescott, the morning dee jay at CD 101.9 in New York, said "Hi" to me on the air that morning. "Good morning to my friend Vernice Watson, living large in New York

City," she bantered. Nothing could burst my bubble that day.

The meeting was held at SA& B's New York office at 1270 Avenue of the Americas. When I walked into my lawyers' office it was impressive. It looked like a big time New York law firm. There were law books all over the place, phones ringing, secretaries buzzing around, and scores of young lawyers in neat little rows of offices. At the end of the long hallway was the conference room. The room had a long conference table and a huge bay window with a dramatic view of Rockefeller Center and the Westside of Manhattan all the way to the Hudson River.

I arrived one hour before the AT&T attorneys were due. There was a spread of food and beverages that looked like it was enough to last all day. Fruit, bagels, pastries, coffee, juice, sodas, bottled water, you name it. I wondered to myself, *Am I paying for all this?*

The lead attorney for my firm was a real pit bull—short and arrogant. Peter Jacobs was good at what he did, and he knew it. He exuded confidence. He sat me down and made sure I was relaxed. Peter had the manner of a doctor who was about to tell you about a difficult procedure. The message was, "We'll make sure you don't feel any pain. Don't worry, you're in good hands."

As Peter started to review the case with me, he told me he did not think that AT&T would offer a settlement that day. "They are coming in to flex their muscles, and they're bringing in a heavy-duty law firm," he warned. He cautioned me not to get upset. "They will try to push your buttons. The other firm's number one goal is to feel you out…see whether or not you would make a good witness." Peter Jacobs closed by saying that he still thought it was a good case. I felt he was sincere. But in the back of my mind, I was wondering if his "we still think it's a good case" was one of his stock lines.

The AT&T lawyers marched in like tin soldiers. I thought the march would never end. First one came through the door, then two, three, four and, finally, five. They sent the ugliest, meanest White lawyers they had to deal with me. I started to muse, *If this is a settlement meeting, why are they sending in so many lawyers?*

Another one of my attorneys, Lester Weiss from Texas, tried to break the ice by saying, "Is this a lawyers' convention?" The "Big Boys" did not crack a smile. I couldn't imagine they were all here for me—the little colored girl from Pikesville. *Why had they sent the big boys, and why so many?*

I was becoming apprehensive, and it started to feel like this was trouble. There were no Black lawyers, not even one spook to sit by the door. There was no pretense that they would go easy on me because I was Black and female. That double minority stuff was right out the window. Usually they would have at least one Black lawyer, perhaps a Black female lawyer to neutralize you. They didn't care about any of that. They might as well have said, *We are White boys all the way, and we came to kick your little black tail!*

My "pit bull" had to leave for a celebrity golf match with a big client. Before they got started, he got up and made his speech. He apologized for having to leave. Then he said very authoritatively, "I want you to know that we believe this is a good case, that we have faith in the case and faith in our client, and that if by the end of the day we have not been able to reach a settlement, we have every intention of taking this case all the way."

Then he was gone. It seemed like a show without its star. He left me with a female attorney and Lester Weiss. It felt like my team was playing the Chicago Bulls in the NBA playoffs, and all my starters were sitting on the bench.

Lester Weiss, the "good ol' boy" from Texas, tried to open up the meeting by commenting that we had received a call from *Bloomberg News* asking about the story. The AT&T lawyers shot him down so fast, it was over before it started. My lawyer punked right out. Before my eyes he shriveled up into a little prune. I knew it was heading downhill. From that point on, AT&T had the floor.

For the next three hours I had to sit there and listen to every Black thing that AT&T had ever done in the history of American Telephone and Telegraph—telling us how "sensitive" AT&T was to Blacks. All of a sudden, there was a little peep from my lawyer in the corner. "Well they couldn't have been that *sensitive* or this 'gorilla' incident never would have happened."

The Big Boys ignored the comment. It was back and forth. They would say something. My lawyers would respond. I felt like I was watching a tennis match. The Big Boys made their intentions quite clear. They said they would drag this out forever and that we would not have the resources to fight them. Revealing their strategy they bragged, "We will go to the judge, motion for a summary judgment, and have your cased dismissed before it ever comes to trial." Now I knew this was no settlement meeting. They were there to intimidate me.

At that point, my lawyers knew I couldn't take anymore. They could see on my face I was devastated. They took me into another room while they went to talk to the Big Boys.

They came back with a figure that was insulting. All my emotions began to leave me. I felt numb. I was back in the bottomless pit. I could feel the life drain out of me. It was hopelessness. I felt as if someone had just ripped my heart right out of my body. They were stealing my dream and getting away with it.

I told my lawyers, "They did not come to settle. Their only purpose was to destroy me, *and this meeting is over!*"

I walked back to the hotel and drank my lunch.

Dismissed

One day I opened my door looking for a check to be delivered by FedEx. A package came, but it was too heavy to be a check. When I opened it, it was from SA&B. It said that the court in New York had granted AT&T's motion and that I could appeal.

All I saw was "DISMISSED." I was paralyzed!

The letter from my lawyers was really wimpy and pitiful. How "disappointed" they were, etcetera. The kicker is that they sent the letter late. When I compared the date on the motion to the date on the letter, I realized that I only had about one week to file a notice of appeal. Then they had the nerve to say they could file an appeal, but I had to pay them $8,000.

I was losing my mind. I didn't have that kind of money! I was trying to mentally and emotionally reconcile my image of AT&T as a fair and just company with that of reality. AT&T was just a big bully that just took and took and took. I was becoming lost, depressed. I felt I was sinking into to a big black bottomless pit. I was doing everything to keep my head above water. *Where was I going to get $8,000?*

I called Lester Weiss at SA&B and left a message with his secretary. He didn't have voice mail. You would think with all that money they make, they would have voice mail. I left a message for him that I was disappointed, that I felt they gave me bad advice, and that I was extremely upset.

I was enraged and I had to get it out. I called Frances in Los Angeles. When Frances' voice mail came on, I could not hold it. I went ballistic on her answering service. I don't even remember all I said. Since Frances is a sister I know I was raw. I told her I thought that SA&B had blown my case.

"...I thought I had some 'good ol' boys' from Texas, but instead I got some wimpy, do-nothing lawyers who went to New York and got emasculated by a bunch of ruthless New Yorkers." My tirade gushed on and on until her machine cut me off.

The next day or so I got two letters from Lester Weiss. One said they were so disappointed in my attitude, they thought they had done a good job and they had put in $90,000 in legal costs. He even said he didn't want to represent me even if I paid. The nerve!

Now I knew I had to get another lawyer, and I told SA&B and Frances so. Then SA&B told me that they would not release the files until I paid them at least $8,000 for expenses. This must have been a PMS week for me because this sent me ballistic again. I'm sorry, but when it's PMS week, I can't always be responsible for my actions.

I called Frances, told her I thought SA&B was trying to sabotage my case by notifying me with only five days left to file an appeal and by blocking me from getting another attorney. There was no way on God's green earth that I was going to continue to do business with these (expletive) low-lifes in suits. I told her that

I was going to the NAACP about SA&B.

In the meantime I cajoled Milton into helping me find a New York lawyer, and he referred me to a ball-busting litigator by the name of Todd K. Rothstein. Everything legal I'd heard about Todd was good. He was good at what he did. He walked the walk and talked the talk. But there was only one problem. He was expensive, and he didn't take cases on contingency. His fee was $15,000.

Now I had two problems. I couldn't afford to pay Todd, and I had to get SA&B to release my case without paying the $8,000. Now that I was thinking more rationally, I called Frances to ask her advice. Apparently, I must have really shaken them up, because Frances told me that Weiss' feelings were hurt, and all he wanted was an apology. I wanted to say, "I'll never apologize." But I knew I had to keep the case moving along and not much time to do it.

Sure enough, Lester Weiss finally caved in after I faxed him an apology. He wrote back that he was releasing my case and waiving the fees.

Hallelujah!

TODD K. ROTHSTEIN

The first time I talked to Todd I liked him. He sounded aggressive. He didn't like the fact that my lawyers waited so long to notify me about the court's decision. I felt good about him. There was hope again. The first thing Todd said he had to do was talk to SA&B.

That's when the mess started again.

Why are lawyers such liars? I thought. When Lester Weiss talked to Todd, he told him at least three out-and-out bold face lies. Lie #1—I had not paid them any money. Lie #2—They had to drag me out of the AT&T settlement meeting kicking and screaming. Lie #3—I had bad-mouthed them all across the country, and they had me on tape. Todd told me all this, and his entire attitude toward me changed. I could not believe it. I was determined not to let these (expletive) lawyers detour my case.

About the first lie, I called SA&B and had them fax me a statement which of course showed several thousand dollars of payments, which I promptly faxed to Todd. About the second lie, I told Todd what really happened and offered him witnesses to back me up.

Regarding lie number three, I called Frances and left a message on her voice mail that I was disappointed she would play a private message from me to her for Lester Weiss. I told her I thought it was a violation of the attorney-client privilege and that I was hurt and disappointed. She called me back and denied it. She even put it in writing and copied Lester Weiss on the letter. Now Lester Weiss had been proven a liar. That was the straw that broke the camel's back. Obviously, Lester Weiss never thought his Jewish brethren would repeat this stuff to the little colored girl from Pikesville. Well, I guess he was wrong. Next!

To make matters worse with me and Todd, I started to have money problems as soon as I got started with him. My preoccupation with AT&T and my ill-advised financing of the Treora Carther and LAC record and video finally caught up with me. But in spite of all that, he filed the appeal.

Our relationship never really got back on track. But I do

know one thing—and it's one of the reasons why I respect Todd—he really likes this case. He thrives on this kind of stuff. He likes going after the big boys and winning big. That's my lawyer. He'll get his money, and I'll get my verdict.

The Colored People

I never really thought about seeking help from the National Association for the Advancement of Colored People (NAACP) until Kweisi Mfume became the national civil rights organization's CEO.

Kweisi Mfume is a very old and dear friend. We had been through so much together in the music business. I planned his surprise birthday party when he was the program director at Morgan State University's radio station WEAA. He emceed the first concert I promoted. I raised money from the music business for his first Congressional campaign.

I automatically figured, *Hey, I've got clout at the NAACP. Maybe I can get Kweisi to pick up the phone and call Robert Allen.* After all, AT&T must give them at least a million dollars a year. And to top it off, Kweisi was the one who wrote the recommendation letter to Robert Allen on my behalf in the first place.

I wrote to my friend. About a week later, I got a letter back from their "assistant general counsel" with some pompous blow-off. I interpreted the response to mean the NAACP only takes on cases they can win and that this was not one of those cases. This was obviously not a PMS week, because it took me a few days to respond. I finally wrote back a very sarcastic response:

Dear Sir:

If I understand you correctly, you appear to be saying that the reason the NAACP cannot assist me is that I did not appeal the June 11, 1996 decision in favor of AT&T.

On the contrary, I did file an appeal, and I am continuing to pursue this most unjust matter. I am pursuing this to the extent that I am looking at over $105,000 in legal fees from three law firms. My business is in jeopardy, and I stand on the verge of financial ruin, all because AT&T decided to steal my ideas and not compensate me for them.

Let me be absolutely clear on what I am requesting of the NAACP. I want President Mfume who, by the way, referred me to AT&T in the first place, to help facilitate a reasonable settlement that will cover my legal costs. I know that Mr. Mfume has a relationship with AT&T, and I know he can get this done. I am not asking for damages, punitive or otherwise. All I want is to be able to recover my legal costs and get on with my life.

Sincerely,
Vernice Watson

It seemed as though I had just turned away from the fax when the phone rang. I'd gotten a callback! It was the Assistant General Counsel on the phone.

I was upset. I asked him, "Do you only take on cases you know you can win? What is the NAACP's role? What do they do? I'm not asking them to take the case to court and fight for me, all I want Kweisi to do is pick up the phone. I'm not some little colored girl off the street, I'm Kweisi's friend. He knows me," I said.

All I was getting was abstract jibber-jabber. I had no idea what he was talking about. Not because it was technical legalese, but because it was drivel. Then he started defending Kweisi by saying he gets thousands of letters and this one was forwarded directly to him, general counsel, and that Kweisi never saw it. As they say on *Seinfeld*, ...*and yadda, yadda, yadda.*

I told him I was going to my network of Black radio stations and tell them how AT&T was screwing me and remind them of the gorilla incident. I was starting to wonder whether this guy was trying to help me or protect AT&T. He told me, "Ms. Watson, you have to be 'careful' about the strategy you use with AT&T."

I have to be "careful" about the strategy I use with AT&T? Now I'm thinking, This boy wouldn't know strategy if it jumped up and slapped him in the face. He couldn't figure out enough strategy to tell somebody how to fight their way out of a wet paper bag.

But here's the kicker.

He actually said, "You have to understand, you are a dwarf. AT&T is a giant."

I started thinking about this "dwarf" business. "Dwarf?" I asked him. "Do you mean one of those little munchkins who followed Snow White around?"

He struggled to eek out a timid, "Yes."

"Well, if that's the case," I said, "Which one am I? Snippy, Dippy, Doopey or Poopy?"

He finally closed out the conversation by giving me the impression he was interested in doing something on the case. He asked that I give Todd permission to discuss the case with him.

THE FRUITCAKE

I wrote Todd giving him permission to discuss the case with the NAACP's general counsel, thinking, *This guy is going to do something.* About a week went by—no word. Milton called his friend Sandra, Todd's secretary, for the 4-1-1. It's nice to have friends on the inside, but sometimes you don't want to hear what they've got to say. And when Milton called me back, what he told me was the last thing I expected to hear.

First of all, this "counsel" never called Todd—Todd called him. When Todd got him on the phone he asked Todd, "Why are you calling me?" Todd, incredulous, answered "I'm calling to discuss Vernice Watson's case against AT&T, per her letter of instruction."

The NAACP's repesentative laughed! He actually laughed at Todd. From what Milton could gather from Sandra, the conversation was all downhill from there.

Assistant Counsel told Todd that the NAACP had no intention whatsoever of getting involved with this case. According to Sandra, he told Todd that I was some kind of fruitcake, that they had dealt with me before, and God knows what else. They talked for a half hour. Sandra summed it up by saying, "There was nothing positive that came out of that conversation."

Milton was mortified. I was in shock. I think Milton was angrier than I was. *The nerve of that guy! Who does he think he is? How could he do such a thing? Why would he do such a thing? This was the NAACP?*

Their handling of my case had given me a new target. The NAACP was in my sights. They had messed with the wrong person this time, and I was out to tear them a new rectal orifice. I was going to cause so much of a ruckus, that Kweisi would be forced to deal with it. The first thing I did was write a scathing letter to Myrlie Evers, the NAACP Board Chairperson:

>...[the assistant general counsel] contacted my attorney, describing me as 'some kind of lunatic,' stating that he had had previous dealings with me and that the 'NAACP had no intention of getting involved.'
>
>I have never requested assistance from the NAACP before, and I certainly have had no contact with Mr. [assistant general counsel] before I sent my letter to Mr. Mfume. I have become very angry with [assistant general counsel] because of the way he talked to me on the phone and the way he talked about me to my attorney.
>
>The NAACP I know has always been the champion of those of us who would otherwise have no hope. And we certainly would not expect to be humiliated and slandered by your staff.
>
>This cannot be the NAACP of W.E.B. Dubois, Roy Wilkins, Ruby Hurley and Medgar Evers. This is not the NAACP that I have known and respected....

The second thing I did was call Vernon Simms, Kweisi's former campaign manager, who's had Kweisi's ear. We were trying to figure this guy out. *He didn't know me, didn't know Todd. Why did he do that? Was he stupid? Tripping? Or just a plain old fool?* Vernon said he would call Kweisi to let him know what was happening.

Last, I called the assistant general counsel to ask if he had spoken to my attorney, to which he replied in the affirmative. But the rest of the conversation was unintelligible. I have no idea what this man said. I did, however, specifically ask him to summarize his telephone conversation with Todd *in writing.* That was the last time I spoke to their legal "counsel."

Then I got a call from *the* General Counsel, Michael Rodgers. He told me he was the boss and that he had been asked by "the corporate office" to give me a call. He asked several innocuous questions that obviously let me know he did not have a clue. I started to think, *What is going on?* Had Vernon gotten hold of Kweisi, or did the poo-poo hit the fan from another direction.

The next call I got was from Kweisi's car phone.

KWEISI TO THE RESCUE

I had hoped to write an exciting end to this chapter—about my old dear friend Kweisi truly coming to my rescue. Unfortunately, it did not happen.

I must admit I was sorely disappointed. I was there for him when his father passed. I was there for him when he was trying to get the respect of the record industry. I was there for him when it came time for him to make the transition from radio to public office. I was there for him when it came time to raise record industry money for his campaign.

But when I needed him the most he was not there for me.

When I told Kweisi what happened, he expressed a great deal of anger. He said he was going to have the man in his office at 9 A.M. the following morning. He said, "I'm sick and tired of this ——, and I'm going to fire him." It never happened.

That was the last time I spoke to Kweisi Mfume. I left him more messages and mailed him copies of documents. For six months, I tried to get his help, to no avail. I finally wrote him this letter. I doubt I'll be hearing from him any time soon.

Personal and Confidential
March 25, 1997

Kweisi Mfume, President & CEO
National Association for the Advancement of Colored People
4805 Mount Hope Drive
Baltimore, MD 21215

Dear Kweisi:

    I never thought the day would come when I would have to say that "I'm disappointed in my friend, Kweisi."

    The last time we talked, you were so outraged by my treatment at the hands of [NAACP Assistant General Counsel], that you told me he was to be in your office by 9 a.m. the next day and that he would be fired. [He] is still there. The man who ridiculed me to my attorney, the man who belittled me, laughed at my case and made me out to be some kind of lunatic is still there at the NACCP. Is this the kind of legal representation you want in your organization?

    Then you give me to Michael Rodgers, who gives great lip-service, but no action. He never responded to my letter of December 23, 1996, asking him to clarify what the NAACP's role would or would not be in my case. This would have been the perfect out for him. He could have responded saying that the NAACP could not pursue it, but instead he ignored me. The only thing he did was call my attorney in New York and tell him to have us stop calling his office. Is this the kind of service that you want the NAACP to provide?

    And finally there's the book. My book will be published. We already have interest from several publishers. The first two chapters in the book, "The Dwarf versus the Giant" and "The Lawyers," are all about my case with AT&T. In fact, "The Dwarf vs. the Giant" is a quote that came directly from your [assistant general counsel]. The second chapter concludes with the cliffhanger "Kweisi to the Rescue." Now I'll have to change that to tell the true story of how the NAACP not only did not help me, but how they ruined my relationship with my attorney and therefore my case.

The NAACP I know has always been the champion of those of us who would otherwise have no hope. And I certainly would not expect to be humiliated and slandered by your staff. This cannot be the NAACP of W.E.B. Dubois, Roy Wilkins, Ruby Hurley and Medgar Evers. This is not the NAACP that I have known and respected.

Kweisi, I hope you don't disappoint me anymore.

Sincerely,
Vernice

THE APPEAL

April 16, 1997. I had just gotten a call from Todd Rothstein's office. I simply told Sandra, "Tell Todd to do whatever he feels like doing. If he feels like this case is good enough to go after AT&T, I'll give him 45 percent."

That's what I would have had to give the other lawyers anyway. Instead of his $15,000 fee, I'd give him 45 percent of whatever the case brought. I thought that might give him the motivation to call AT&T to cut a deal or whatever. I said, "The bottom line is that I have no more money. I'm working three jobs: I'm working for my own company; I'm working for Ryland Homes selling houses; and I have a job from 4:45 until midnight selling MBNA $100,000 credit cards."

I told her, "I cannot put any more money into this case. Unless a miracle happens between now and June, I don't see $15,000 to pay a lawyer to continue this fight," I said. "Tell Todd to do whatever he wants."

Hindsight is 20-20. If I knew then what I know now, I would never be fighting AT&T. If my first attorney had given me a realistic overview of what I would have to go through, I would not be sitting here with my company near bankruptcy and working three jobs just to pay off this debt. I had neglected my company, and I couldn't do that anymore.

April 21, 1997. I spoke to Todd and repeated the offer I made to his secretary. As soon as I said, "I'll pay you 45 percent," he put me on hold. Attorneys always do that so they can round up witnesses to hear a deal. We agreed that I would pay expenses up to one thousand dollars and 45 percent of whatever he collected from AT&T.

April 25, 1997. Todd K. Rothstein filed the Appeal in the Supreme Court of the State of New York, Appellate Division, on Friday, April 25, 1997.

Now AT&T is on *my* time. The Appeal process will take at least another year or so, and by then my book will be out.

Next!

Chapter 5

Epilogue

PRESTIGE

Fast forward to 1998....My last "job" was at Light Records in 1985. Ever since then, I've been on my own. After I left Light, Prestige & Associates began to grow, and I haven't looked back since.

I have represented a number of gospel and crossover artists: Whitney Houston, Aretha Franklin, Deniece Williams, The Winans, BeBe & CeCe Winans, Candi Staton, James Cleveland, The Clark Sisters, Yolanda Adams, The Gospel Keynotes, Stephanie Mills, Darryl Coley, Fred Hammond, The O'Jays, Phil Driscoll, Howard Hewett, Milton Brunson, Kathleen Battle, Tramaine Hawkins, Mariah Carey, Kirk Whalum, Oleta Adams, Richard Smallwood Singers, Bobby Jones, Doug Miller, The Williams Brothers, Commissioned, Mighty Clouds of Joy, Myrna

Summers, Inger Reid, D.J. Rogers, Witness, Michael Speaks, Rance Allen, Ben Tankard, John P. Kee, and The Sounds of Blackness.

South Africa

There have been many perks, too. It wasn't *all* hard work. So far I've hit four continents. I've been to London several times. I've been to MIDEM, the largest international music conference in Cannes France—twice. I've been to Mexico, South America and South Africa. Perhaps the most memorable trip was South Africa.

The trip was a fact-finding mission by a group of African American media professionals. Nobody wanted me to go to South Africa. Everybody tried to talk me out of it because Nelson Mandela was still in jail. My argument was we basically believe the media hype, whatever is in the papers or on television. And we believe it without investigating. The truth of the matter was, it was a free first-class trip, and I wanted to go. It wasn't about going back to the motherland to check out my roots. It was more about me developing my business beyond the borders of the good old USA.

The trip lasted a wonderful two weeks. Ten of us flew British Airways from Dulles to London and then South African Airways to Johannesburg. Arriving at the SAA terminal at Heathrow, we got our first taste of *apartheid*—they body searched us. These South Africans did not remind us of anyone from Alabama. They were worse! They looked at us with disdain, as if we were dirt!

When we landed at Johannesburg, they got around the passport prohibition by stamping some documents instead of our passports. We never went through customs. When we got off the 747, we walked across the tarmac to a waiting Lear Jet to take us the rest of the way to Bophuthatswana and Sun City. Sun City made Las Vegas look like Walbrook Junction.

I must admit business had been good—until I ran into the two-headed monster that was the AT&T lawsuit and the Treora Carther production.

Verlen Music

In an attempt to diversify my interests, I tried my hand at artist management and music publishing. Publishing was a great idea. Management turned out to be a real fiasco. I heard someone say in a music conference somewhere that the number one quality you have to have as a manager is undying and uncompromising belief in your artist. Whoever said that left out two key elements—patience and money—one of which I had little of, the other I was not willing to wait for.

My first client was Billie Sanders. Things went well at first, until I ran out of those two precious resources, patience and money. I have to tell you, lack of patience and money will make you forget "undying and uncompromising belief" any day.

I get a $25 check from Billie every month for life for the money she owes me. It probably won't be paid back until my grandson's first year in college. But the bright side of it is, I just got a publisher's royalty check for $3.73 from the Republic of South Africa. I told you publishing was *good business!*

Ronny Chantal was another case. Ronny is one of the most

talented songwriters and producers in the industry. He's produced cuts on Najee, Alex Bunyon and one of the biggest gospel projects, *Kingdom*. As part of my management deal with Ronny, I took him around New York and used my considerable clout to walk him into the offices of the top Black music executives.

Ronny Chantal would never have been able to get an audience with Senior Vice President Doug Daniel at Arista, Senior Vice President Tony Anderson at Sony, or Senior Vice President Glynice Coleman at Capitol EMI. I even took him to the annual Gospel Music Association Convention in Nashville to meet the gospel music bigwigs. As a direct result of my efforts, he got a deal with Benson Records in Nashville.

What did Vernice get for her efforts? Nothing—absolutely nothing. All I got was empty promises from Ronny Chantal.

I have a sign sitting over my desk that says, *Out of every adversity comes a seed for greater or equal opportunity.* I must admit, sometimes I feel like tearing that sign off the wall and running over it with my Lexus. But there is a lot of truth in that statement. Through my experience with Ronny Chantal, I met John Smith. When I was in New York, taking Ronny around to the record companies, producer Leland Holly (another so-called friend turned bad), stopped by my hotel, The Morgan, to introduce me to John Smith.

The Morgan was an odd sort of place. It is very exclusive, and it caters to European business types. It doesn't even have a sign or a marquee, just these black glass doors. Everything is black and neon. And everyone there, guests included, seemed to be wearing black. So I decided to wear white.

One Thing Leads To Another

John Smith is a wonderful producer, songwriter and musician. But most importantly, John is a good friend. He taught me so much about production. He produced my first and last real production, Treora Carther and The L. A. Chorale. John is the only management client I had who actually paid me a 15% commission. He was also responsible for bringing me my last management client, an incredibly talented singer with incredibly bad judgment, Norma Joy.

John recently appeared on the *Ricki Lake* show for a surprise marriage proposal to his girlfriend Lisa in front of her doubtful mother and a national television audience. I got a true reminder of my friendship with John while I was watching that show. The picture that was shown of John and Lisa was one I took of them at my annual Fourth of July cookout. Thank God for John Smith.

The Production

In 1992 I met Treora Carther through Leland Holly. Treora had a publishing problem with John Ashe at Word Records. I stepped in and solved the problem. Treora and I became friends and I became her manager.

When the spring of 1995 came, and I was in the midst of my preoccupation with AT&T. Many of my promotion accounts had fallen by the wayside due to lack of attention. Promotion accounts are like plants; you have to give them water, sunlight and attention, or they'll wither away. It's the same thing with records. If you don't nurture them, your records will fall off the charts, and your clients will disappear. It was time for a new album for Treora.

I had been working on a deal to finance a record to be recorded live during the annual Gospel Music Workshop of America Convention, which was to be held in Los Angeles that August. For Treora and the L. A. Chorale it would be the perfect situation. I promised Treora she would have her live recording in Los Angeles. As the AT&T debacle wore on, I became more and more emotionally involved in the live recording. The LAC project was becoming sort of a counter balance to my AT&T obsession.

Under the guidance of John Smith, the project's producer, we worked out all the preproduction details—song selections, sound trucks, venues, musicians. I even made a deal to bring in Howard Hewett to lead on the song *He's My Rock*.

I pulled out all the stops. I sent invitations to everybody who was anybody in the world of gospel to come to our recording. I knew I was doing a good job as Executive Producer. I had the best songs, the best musicians, the best soloist, and to tie it all together, I had the best producer in John Smith.

In spite of all the preparation, there was one thing that no one could have prepared me for—*my financial partner dropping out*. Three weeks before the recording, my financial partner and distributor, a guy who owned an independent distribution company, backed out of the project.

I was devastated. There was nowhere to go for financing on that short a notice. Yet, I could not cancel. We had gone too far. I had invited everyone in the business, and I could not let Treora down.

I turned to the only friends I had. They were all in my safe at home, and I never touched them. They were Citibank Visa Gold, American Express Platinum and three of their friends. I ran up $70,000 in charges to pay for this project. At the same time I called out the calvary—all of my friends to help me manage the project and keep costs down. What I didn't know was that bringing in Milton Allen to handle the video and line produce, and Eilene Lifesy-Towns to handle everything else, would end up costing me more money.

It was worth having Milton and Eilene there. They kept me from going crazy and succumbing to the pressure. It may have cost me, but it ran smooth as silk.

Treora is a great choir director, but she's no singer. She insisted on singing the lead on the title song medley, *For He Knows Me*. I'll never forget how during the recording John left his perch directing the band, came over to me and whispered in my ear, "We'll have to do something about this."

Whenever you do something "live," things are bound to go wrong. We had planned on recording *He's My Rock* twice that night. We knew that would be our hit. Howard Hewett had to catch a plane and that forced us to change the order of the recording. Now we only had one take to do *He's My Rock*. And sure as Murphy's Law is Murphy's Law, Howard Hewett forgot the second verse. He did a great job of ad-libbing, but he only left me with half a song.

Finally, my other big A&R contribution to the project was one of my favorite songs, Andrae Crouch's *I'll Be Thinking of You*. I even arranged to bring in Kristle Murden who did the original song, and Howard Smith flew in from Detroit. By the time they were ready to perform, Howard Smith was so intimidated by the overwhelming power of the choir, he just couldn't pull it off. He had a terrible performance.

We were scheduled to record *I'll Be Thinking of You* twice that night, but Howard Smith used every excuse in the book, from his voice being raw, to his plane ticket being wrong. The bottom line was, in the words of my associate producer Michael Soward, "He just didn't have it."

I was so upset by their performance I was ready to scrap the whole song until my friend Patti Howard, a background singer for Whitney Houston and a great songwriter and producer, comforted me.

I said, "How could they ruin my favorite song? That was the one I was waiting all night to hear."

Patti said to me, "Vernice, whatever you do, do not scratch this song. The choir is slamming, the tracks are hot. Just go back into the studio and overdub the lead vocals."

I respected Patti's opinion, and I was determined to salvage that song. I realized that Howard and Kristle were trying to play me. They actually used their poor performance to try to convince me to let them rerecord their vocals in a studio and produce the track. After their performance and the way they let me down that night, I wouldn't let them produce their way out of a wet paper bag.

Another thing about live recordings is when things go wrong, you can usually fix them in the studio. And in the studio is where John is the master. He overdubbed Norma Joy's lead vocal on Treora's *For He Knows Me*. Norma's vocals took that song from a throwaway to a potential hit single.

On *I'll Be Thinking Of You*, John kept Kristle Murden's signature line and brought in budding vocalists Jeff Graham and

Sherry McGhee. Sherry McGhee took over that song! The day FedEx delivered the tape to me, it was in the midst of a major snowstorm. I had just put the tape on when my friend Wayne Cooper, a guitarist for the Basement Boyz, walked through the front door. When he heard the new mix, he dropped to his knees and said over and over, "John is ba-d-d! The brother is badd!"

The album turned out great, but the fact that I had to substitute Norma Joy's vocal for Treora's never sat quite well with the LAC Chorale leader. Even though it significantly improved the project and made it much more marketable, it marked the beginning of the end of my relationship with Treora Carther.

We eventually turned Verlen Music into a marketing company. To this day we are still getting returns on Treora Carther's record. I still haven't recovered my money. I'm still $50,000 in debt.

NORMA JOY

After the release of *For He Knows Me* on the LAC album with Norma's lead, John and I began to pull songs together for Norma. She would be the next Verlen Music production. My strategy was to use Treora's record as a vehicle to promote Norma while we were preparing her recording project. It was a good strategy. Generate momentum from the LAC project to get a buzz going on Norma, then release her record and ride the crest of the wave.

I knew this would work because Norma has a distinctive voice with a lot of depth. She's extremely talented and as I was about to find out, extremely hardheaded.

It was January of 1997, and the record industry had just gone through one of the worst fourth quarters in recent memory. On the gospel side, the top 20 records sold through, and the major distributors who had marketing clout were able to hold their own. But the small independents like me were faced with boxes upon boxes of returned merchandise. I wasn't a happy camper that January day when I got an unexpected call from Laine Delaney.

Laine had been a good friend who had headed three major gospel labels, all of which had received hefty administrative and marketing support from the corporate parents. At the time there were six major distributors—WEA, Polygram, Capitol-EMI, BMG, SONY, and MCA/Universal—all of which made, at one time or another, some kind of foray into gospel music. Laine always seemed to end up heading one of those labels. She pretty much hired me everywhere she went. I helped put her promotion and marketing teams together.

I worked all Laine's records, and I brought street level credibility to her and her corporate benefactors. Laine is one of the most resilient music executives I have ever known. Despite her last two corporate-backed labels going bust, she always manages to bounce back.

Laine was calling that day to let me know that another one of the majors and a large independent were combining forces to create a new gospel label, Lance Records. She would be the General Manager. She told me about the artists she was signing. They were all marquee names in gospel music—well known artists with established track records. One artist in particular was recognized as a driving force in gospel music over the last 25 years.

She wanted me to start in April when her first release hit the street. I had worked for Laine before, and I believed her to be a friend. For those reasons, I took her at her word and *verbally* agreed to her terms—a decision I would later regret.

By the end of February, John Smith had already recorded eight demo songs on Norma Joy. I got a call from Norma telling me that producer Leland Holly had been working with her and wanted to sign her to a recording deal backed by Dave Chiarchiaro, the owner of a New York jingle and commercial production house.

I greeted this news with mixed emotion. For Norma, Leland and Chiarchiaro I kept on my game face, talking about contracts, deal points and how great and wonderful Norma was. John was upset that it appeared as though all his work was going for nothing. Privately, I was ambivalent. I really wanted to record Norma, especially considering the wonderful work that John had done with her.

But my practical side, which usually wins out, told me I was tapped out. I had spent so much on the recording, manufacturing, packaging and marketing of Treora Carther that it would be a relief if Dave Chiarchiaro could offer her a deal. There is one thing that bothered me about this whole business. Why did Norma wait so long to tell him about this? Why did she hide the offer from John?

LANCE RECORDS

By mid March we had started pre-promoting Lance product. The first release was by a well established choir director, produced by none other than Leland Holly. The second was a gospel album by a classy jazz stylist. Things were looking up. I knew Lance Records would help me attract other clients. Chiarchiaro would take on the financial burden of recording Norma. Meanwhile, I would continue to dig myself out of the hole that I dug for myself with the LAC project.

I called my attorney E. Scott Johnson at Ober, Kaler, Grimes & Shriver and told him that I did not want to spend a lot of money in attorney's fees to negotiate Norma's contract with Chiarchiaro. E. Scott advised me how to proceed on each deal point, and I followed his directions to the letter. After that, we had the conference call with Chiarchiaro, Leland Holly, Milton and myself to finalize all the deal points.

Everyone agreed on all the points. I sent the contract off to Norma for her review and execution. Curiously, we didn't hear from Norma right away. In fact we didn't hear from her in quite a while. I thought maybe she changed her mind. For me, no news was good news from Norma Joy. Besides, I was busy working hard for my new client, Lance Records.

GOOD NEWS AND BAD NEWS

Two months went by and I finally heard from Norma Joy. "Vernice, I have good news and bad news for you. Which do you want first?" she said.

I, of course, said, "Give me the bad news first." To which she insisted on giving me the good news.

"Here's the good news. Have you ever heard of Lance Records?"

"Yes," I said. "I have a two-year contract with them."

Without even considering any potential conflict in what I had just said she continued, "Well, I have a contract with them."

"Ok, then. What's the bad news?" I asked.

Norma responded, "The bad news is that I have to fire you as my manager. The producer and the record company do not want you as my manager."

The shock was just sinking in when I politely said, "Norma, I wish you all the luck in the world."

She couldn't believe how calm and collected I was. She even said that she wanted me to scream at her because she felt so guilty. I wished her luck and got off the phone as fast as I could.

When I hung up that phone I was absolutely seething. I was breathing fire. A dizzying array of thoughts went through my head. I could not believe that Leland Holly, Laine Delaney and Norma Joy could stab me in the back so blatantly. Then again Norma was so hardheaded and so gullible, I could see how she let them manipulate her. How did they expect to get away with this? Why didn't Vincent, whom I helped get the job as Laine's marketing coordinator, warn me? What was going on?

My first instinct was to call Laine at home and go ballistic on her. But instead I settled for the safer route of chewing out Vincent to find out what he knew and when he knew it. I called Vincent and went off on him. I told him it was a question of loyalty—loyalty to an old friend or loyalty to your current employer. The paycheck people won, and the best I could get out of Vincent was ambivalent denials.

But he did say two things that comforted me somewhat. Number one, he was not a part of it, and he refused to get involved with it based on his friendship with me. Secondly, he asked me a question that made me sit back and consider some other options.

"Don't you have a valid management agreement with Norma Joy?"

Vincent queried.

Yes, I did. And I decided my strategy would be to keep that contract in force until after she signed her agreement with Lance.

Vincent called me the moment she signed the contract. I called Norma at home that evening to find out how soon I'd be getting my 15 percent. Norma was acting particularly nervous and evasive that night. She claimed she didn't even know the amount of her advance. How can you sign a recording contract, the most valued thing in your life, and not know how much you're getting paid?

I believed Norma was lying to me. I didn't have time for that kind of nonsense.

The next day I called Laine. I was in pursuit of my management fee, but I must admit I was in a bit of a mischievous mood. I wanted to push her buttons. I asked Laine how she wanted to handle my management fee and whether she wanted me to send her a Letter of Direction. A Letter of Direction instructs a record company where to direct various payments due an artist, management or production company.

Laine went nuts. She started yelling and screaming at me. I was just as cool and calm as a cucumber. Laine was a fat cat in a do-nothing job, and I was not scared of her in the least. Her argument was that I did not have a contract with Norma and, therefore, was not entitled to any of her advance.

I promptly faxed her a 13 page agreement that was still in force.

I gathered from that conversation that Norma had lied to them as well and told them that she had already "fired" me. Laine called the producer and called Norma and evidently cussed them out.

Norma called me crying, "Why are you doing this to me?"

I hung up on her. Norma was typical of many artists in that she wanted it so bad, she would sacrifice anybody and anything in the process to get what she wanted. As much as I respected Norma's talent, I quietly hoped to myself that she gets what she deserves.

They waited until after they got my database and mailing labels, without which they could not have gotten off square one. They waited until I had launched the label, did their listening party for the jazz artist and brought the record in on *Billboard's* chart to debut at #5 before they started their dirty work. I expected it. I just did not know when it would come. But I knew once they started, my timing would be everything.

I received a one-line termination letter from Norma Joy. This, too, did not surprise me, because according to our agreement, I was still her manager for 90 days after she serves me notice. I suspect that Norma had probably lost the contract agreement and probably did not realize the terms. Milton and I were prepared for these contingencies, and we had previously gone through all my files and expenses and composed a bill for Norma totaling $30,000. I timed the delivery of the letter so she would receive it just before she had to perform for Lance Records at the annual Gospel Music Workshop of America Convention that August. I wanted her to look me in the face while she was performing, and I wanted her to think about that $30,000 and everything I did for her ungrateful self.

The people at Lance were trying to act normal at the GMWA, but it was clear that they were very uneasy with me. I knew it was only a matter of time before my relationship with Lance would end. I just wanted to be paid for my database, my Lance contract and my management fees.

When I got back home there was a letter from Norma's lawyer (I wonder who was paying that bill?) stating that she owed me nothing. This made me even more angry and recalcitrant. We responded to her lawyer with one of the most eloquent letters that Milton and I have ever composed:

August 18, 1997

[address omitted]
Re: Norma Joy

Dear Mr. Glass:

Let me be perfectly clear and frank about how I view this latest debacle with Norma Joy. First of all, in reference to the fax I sent: I was not trying to justify any claim or submit any documents "evidencing the expenses claimed" in connection with the services I provided to Norma Joy. The purpose of those documents is to evidence to you that I have acted as Norma Joy's manager and representative over the last four years.

With specific regard to the draft July 1996 agreement, the intent is to demonstrate to you that we did the work and negotiated the deal with Dave Chiarchiaro and Leland Holly. As an attorney, I am sure you are familiar with the time, professional fees and legal fees that accompany such work. I was never reimbursed for my time or expenses which include attorney's fees.

Mr. Glass, I suggest you talk to your client and try to get a look at the big picture here as far as her career is concerned:

1. Norma Joy would not be where she is today, had it not been for my contacts, reputation and consistent good faith work ethic to move Norma's career along. I introduced her to Laine Delaney, the general manager of Lance Records and architect of Norma's recording contract. In 1995, while suffering in the midst of a back injury, I came to New York with an assistant for the express purpose of bringing Laine Delaney to see Norma Joy perform. There are costs associated with this activity including two AMTRAK tickets, lodging, food and the cost of paying my assistant to go to New York. Like in the previous paragraph, I was never reimbursed for my time or expenses. Most of theses points are outlined in my letter to Norma of May 23, 1997. I would suggest you refamiliarize yourself with that document.

2. I am currently contracted by Lance Records to coordinate and execute national promotion for all Lance Records product. This, of course, includes the national promotion effort for Norma's release. My first directive on the Norma Joy project is to set up a national promotion tour for her. I intend to execute my duties for Lance Records on behalf of Norma in good faith as I have always done, but I would expect some good faith from your client in return.

3. If you ask anyone in the gospel music industry, you will most likely find that I have a sterling reputation for doing good thorough work and treating people fairly. I do not believe I am being treated fairly by your client. I have no ill feelings toward Norma, and I still would like to see the fruition of my labor on Norma's behalf.

4. Is she denying that I acted as her agent and manager over the last four years? The expenses I summarized are meager compared to the impact my efforts have had on Norma's career. Does she deny this? Even at her recent performance at the Gospel Music Workshop of America in Cincinnati, Norma never acknowledged Prestige during her remarks. This evoked a curious reaction among the gospel industry elite who questioned her omission. Even the Chairman of the Gospel Announcer's Guild mentioned her omission. Does she think she did it on her own? If that is the case then she is delusional

and you sir are having the proverbial wool pulled over your eyes.

Mr. Glass, singers like Norma Joy come and go. Record labels come and go. It is relationships that endure in the music industry. This is why I have been so successful over the last twenty years. My specialty is breaking new talent, and I have worked with the top gospel and crossover singers at the inception of their careers including, Yolanda Adams, Tramaine Hawkins, CeCe Winans, Vanessa Bell Armstrong, Anita Baker and Whitney Houston. To put it bluntly, there's no one that can do it better. That's why Norma and I got together in the first place.

As far as money is concerned, twelve thousand four hundred fifty-seven dollars ($12,457.00) in expenses over four years is surely a bargain. Eighteen thousand dollars ($18,000.00) in professional fees over a four year period? This figure does not even begin to compensate me for the time and effort I put into Norma Joy. If we were to calculate my work for Norma at my hourly rate as most attorney's do, the figure would be out of sight.

Mr. Glass, my question for your client is, "What value does she put on the services I provided for her?" I would think the value to her would far exceed any of the figures we have discussed. I would like to know what value Norma places on my four painstaking and thankless years of involvement with her career and her personal life? Whatever figure she comes up with, I will consider for its settlement value.

As of today, I will be on vacation for 10 days. Immediately upon my return I will begin to finalize arrangements for Norma's promotional tour. I have no time to nitpick over a paltry sum that does not nearly come close to genuinely compensating me for the effort I put out on Norma's behalf. My accountant is Joan Pratt, the duly elected Comptroller of Baltimore City. My attorneys are E. Scott Johnson of Ober, Kaler Grimes & Shriver of Baltimore and Tab K. Rosenfeld of Perlman, Rosenfeld & Jacobs of New York. I have no intention of tying up their time and resources and my money on this matter.

Find out what it's worth to your client and get back to me. If you can not reach me, feel free to contact my business associate Milton Allen in my office.

A final word. In consideration of the comments I made about relationships in this very small industry. What kind of reputation does Norma want to have as she begins her career? Does she want to have an acrimonious and distrusting relationship with the very person who not only got her career going, but is charged with the duty of promoting her first record? Or...does she want to be reasonable, productive and cooperative? The choice is hers. My professional credibility and reputation cannot be impugned. Norma Joy still has hers to earn.

Sincerely,
Vernice Watson

cc: E. Scott Johnson, Ober, Kaler, Grimes & Shriver
     Tab K. Rosenfeld, Perlman, Rosenfeld & Jacobs
     Laine Delaney, Lance Records

Dictated but not read.
VW/mba

I made sure that the letter was sent to everyone and that it was received two days before our weekly conference call. I would be able to gauge their reaction to my bombshell from the call. Sure enough, as soon as they started the conference call with their phony prayer, I knew it was all over. They practically ignored me on the call. As soon as it was over, I got a fax saying that my services for Lance Records would no longer be required.

This all flowed from Laine Delaney, someone whom I thought was a friend, someone that I was loyal to, someone that I taught the business to, and finally, someone who was my employer. I allowed her to take credit for my work. After all those years of service to Laine, this is what I get—not just a knife in the back with Norma, but impaled by the theft of my database and used, abused and trampled by the termination of my livelihood and the trashing of my reputation.

My lawyers told me that it would cost thousands of dollars to file suit and even then, I'm not guaranteed a victory. After AT&T, I decided no more lawyers, no more lawsuits. I'll take my losses and move on.

All my friends will tell you about the depression I sank into during the fall of 1997. I thought I was keeping up a good front. But the losses from the LAC recording, the betrayal of Norma Joy, the Lance Records calamity, and the constant haranguing by creditors was more than I could take. I began to lose faith.

I couldn't do it anymore. I had given my best to gospel music for the last twenty years. My faith had been shattered. With tears in my eyes, I prayed:

Lord, if I have to deal with heathens, then I would rather not be involved with gospel music...I would rather go back to the secular side. God, I need to hear from you.

Later that day, I got a call from the most powerful woman in the gospel music industry today—Vicki Mack Lataillade, the President and CEO of Gospo Centric Records. Maybe, just maybe, I can get there from here.